Working with Guides and Angels

Working with Guides and Angels

Ruth White

PIATKUS

ஃ *Visit the Piatkus website!*

Piatkus publishes a wide range of bestselling fiction and non-fiction, including books on health, mind, body & spirit, sex, self-help, cookery, biography and the paranormal.

If you want to:
- read descriptions of our popular titles
- buy our books over the internet
- take advantage of our special offers
- enter our monthly competition
- learn more about your favourite Piatkus authors

VISIT OUR WEBSITE AT: www.piatkus.co.uk

Copyright © 1996 by Ruth White

First published in Great Britain in 1996 by
Piatkus Books Ltd
5 Windmill Street, London W1T 2JA
email: info@piatkus.co.uk

Reprinted 1996, 1997, 1998, 1999, 2000, 2001 (twice), 2002, 2003, 2004

This edition published in 2006

The moral right of the author has been asserted

A catalogue record for this book is available from the British Library

ISBN 0 7499 2754 2

Edited by Carol Franklin
Designed by Sue Ryall

This book has been printed on paper manufactured
with respect for the environment using wood from
managed sustainable resources

Printed and bound in Great Britain by Antony Rowe Ltd,
Chippenham, Wiltshire

To Mary Swainson,
with love and gratitude

ACKNOWLEDGEMENTS

My love and thanks go to: my friends for their tolerance and understanding; my daughter Jane for her love and support; my dog Jackson for his companionship as I write; Tony Van den Bergh for unstinting help with the manuscript; the angels and guides, particularly Gildas, for the extra dimension they bring to life.

CONTENTS

CONTENTS

Exercises

PROLOGUE

Since early childhood I have been accompanied by a shining presence. At first I thought this being was an angel. During childhood I was lonely and this being was a wonderful companion and inner playmate. When I was nineteen I recognised that he was my discarnate guide. He asked me to call him Gildas and began to prepare me for our serious work together. He has now communicated with me on a daily basis for over 38 years.

It is exciting to have such a presence always near but it also brings responsibilities. Knowing Gildas has shaped and changed my life. His teachings have been translated into several different languages. Many people now come to me so that I can channel Gildas's wisdom for their lives and dilemmas.

The full story of our relationship is told in *Gildas Communicates*, and is updated in: *A Question of Guidance*; *Working With Your Chakras*; *A Message of Love*, and *The River of Life* (see Bibliography).

My experience of guides, angels, other dimensions, auras, nature spirits, fairies, energy fields and energetic healing was difficult to talk about almost 40 years ago. This is not so now. The veil between the different planes of experience is growing thinner. An increasing number of people see angels and hear guides or long to do so. For many the pressing questions are, 'How can I use this experience?' 'What will it mean in my life?' Or, 'How can I increase my perception of other worlds?' 'How can I welcome guides and angels into my life?'

It is unwise to explore other planes and dimensions without self-knowledge. The best pathway to the world of discarnate beings first takes in sound psychological insights in order to gather the innate wisdom of the psyche. My own journey led me to study the art of self growth and counselling with particular reference to the transpersonal psychologies of Jung, Maslow and Assagioli. (Transpersonal psychology is the study of human nature and behaviour which lays particular emphasis on spiritual aspiration and the search for higher meaning in life.)

Guides and angels want to be our loving companions and supporters. They encourage us to widen our viewpoint. All too often, consciously or unconsciously, we turn them into judgemental critics and moralists, denigrating ourselves and investing them with a power *over* us which they do not seek. In order to clear and lighten our relationship with them and to be able to explore the other worlds with safety, self-growth and discovery must be undertaken.

This book, then, speaks of guides and angels and gives suggestions for how you can work with and know them. It also lays emphasis on the need to recognise those of our limitations and preconceptions which can *colour* and influence contact with other worlds and cause false messages or impressions to be received.

We live in challenging times. Each day the media confronts us with violence, pathos and pain. If you are eager not to lose touch with joy, laughter and celebration, if you feel in danger of losing hope or powerless as a tiny drop in a turbulent ocean, learning to work with guides and angels can be the catalyst you need.

Beings of light are supporting humanity as we face the struggle to break through into greater potential. Working with them restores trust in the universe, decreases our loneliness and enhances our quality of life.

If you want to play a part in bringing about major personal and collective spiritual change, you are ready to be

working with the guides and angels who are eager to build
a bridge of light between the different planes of consciousness. This book will help you on your way.

1

FROM REALMS OF LIGHT

Perceiving other worlds ... Extra-sensory perception ... What do we know about the realms of light? ... Personal experience of other worlds ... Guides and angels ... Gildas ... Temples of light ... Reincarnation ... Higher guides ... Gildas's identity ... Do we all have a personal guide and angel? ... Exercise 1.

Perceiving other worlds

As children, we are taught that we are on earth and God is in heaven. Since 'heaven', 'the heavens', 'sky' and 'the skies' are used as synonyms, we come to think of God as being above us, actually living somewhere in the sky. Many young children, flying in an aeroplane for the first time, expect – and fear! – to see God or angels in the clouds. Because of this concept, many of us, when thinking of loved ones who have died, almost instinctively glance up at the heavens.

These early explanations make it difficult to understand the concept that 'heaven', or the higher vibrational spheres, surround us and are hidden only by a 'veil' in our perceptions. When that veil lifts or parts we get a glimpse of other worlds or planes with infinite vistas. These exhilarating moments happen to ordinary people in the everyday course of life much more often than may generally be suspected.

It is not necessary for you to be clairvoyant, mediumistic or to have had a 'near-death experience' for the veil to part. When it does, you will know that the other worlds are very close. They have a special and unforgettable quality of light, vastly different from anything you may normally perceive.

Extra-sensory perception

It is the quality of light which sets these experiences apart and makes us recognise that we have had an extra-sensory perception. Even if only for a moment, we have been privileged to glimpse another dimension where life is eternal and beings of light dwell.

The realisation that the veil has parted can be frightening. The reason why most glimpses of other worlds tend to be momentary is because fears of disorientation cause us to close down quickly, and retreat into the known and normal. Immediately afterwards questions arise and fears surface: 'Did that really happen? Have I had an optical illusion? Is there something wrong with my eyes? Am I going mad? What will happen if I step too far into another world and cannot find my way back? If I share this experience with others, even those close to me, will they worry about me or begin to think I am strange? If I tell anyone they'll laugh! Is it possible to get "taken over" or "possessed"? What are these so-called "other worlds" anyway?'

Many of us hide any visionary experiences and secretly worry about them. Yet a doctor in Holland, who made a practice of asking his patients if they had ever seen an angel, had an overwhelming number of affirmative responses. Most people – even if they have not actually 'seen' a being of light – will relate peak experiences: 'Something beautiful was there'; 'A benign and healing presence was caring for me'; 'My guardian angel stepped in'; 'I know I am never alone'; 'I felt as if wings were enfolding me'; 'When I was a child I always saw my angel at the foot of my bed'.

What do we know about the realms of light?

Our knowledge of other worlds and their inhabitants comes from esoteric traditions, mystics, mediums, sensitives, clair-voyants and people who have had out of the body or near-death experiences.

The overwhelming evidence or consensus of opinion is that the other worlds are full of joy, wisdom, non-judgementalism and the previously mentioned quality of light. Many of the beings who dwell there appear, to those who have seen them, to be wearing a garment of light.

My personal experience of other worlds

Since childhood I have been aware of a presence or being who accompanies me everywhere, to whom I can speak and from whom I receive replies which flood into my mind like a form of dictation. When I was very young I thought this presence was an angel, because he wore a white robe and shimmered. I also saw another angelic presence with wings, who shines with rainbow light. I assumed that these were two different kinds of angel. Much later, the being in the white robe told me that his name is Gildas, and that he is a discarnate guide and teacher. The rainbow shimmering being is my guardian angel.

Guides and angels

Guides and angels are from different streams of conscious-ness. Guides are part of the human stream and have been incarnate. Angels are emanations which come directly from the divine source. They have never incarnated and never will. Angels will never become humans and, contrary to a common belief system, humans will never be angels. (See also Chapter 3 for more on this.)

Gildas

Gildas has taught me much about other worlds and has helped me to understand my extra-sensory experiences or extended vision. As a child I could see coloured lights (auras) around people. I saw what I now know to be guardian angels and other angelic presences. I was aware of the nature spirits or fairies at work in the garden, near water, in the flames of the fire and – particularly on windy days – in the air. At first I did not realise that other people could not see these things and as a result I lived in a deeply confusing world. Later I concluded that it was better not to speak of what I saw and eventually I learned to 'tune out' from everything except Gildas.

As I grew older I began to fear that being aware of Gildas's presence and having conversations with him was a sign that I was mad. It was a great relief when, aged 19, I met Mary Swainson, a Jungian therapist who also had esoteric knowledge. Mary reassured me that I was not psychotic but used the word *mediumship*, which I had never heard before. (See also Bibliography: *Gildas Communicates*, for the full story.)

Once I relaxed my state of mind and accepted Gildas's presence as natural, his teachings began to flow. Gradually I learned to tune in again, not all the time, but when I want to. I do not automatically see people's auras now or, as some people imagine, have some kind of X-ray vision so that I know all about them simply by looking! When I give healing or am specifically asked to sense someone's aura or chakras, then I see colours, patterns and activity which I have learned to interpret.

When I am in the garden or some other natural setting I can 'shift level', see the auras of plants and trees, and watch the nature spirits at work.

Gildas has taught me about other worlds and has guided me on journeys to other planes. There are six subtle areas, beyond the physical or material plane. Different esoteric schools have slightly different names for them. Here, they will be referred to as: the etheric, the astral, the feeling, the lower mental, the higher mental and the ketheric planes (listed in ascending order of vibrational rate).

Temples of light

The astral, the feeling and the mental planes have many temples of light and healing. They are constructed of streams of light and colour which interweave to form geometric shapes. For different purposes there are squares, spheres, pyramids and stars. Angels and guides work within these temples, but so also do other helpers. When we die we may work in the light temples and learn about healing. When we are asleep many of us travel to the astral planes to heal ourselves, to dream significant or healing dreams, and to assist in healing and reassuring others.

Reincarnation

You do not have to believe in reincarnation to see and experience other worlds or be able to converse with guides and angels. However, most guides teach that we have lived more than once. The wider perpsective Gildas brings to the problems we experience in being incarnate often refers to other lifetimes and to the concept of karma – the spiritual law of cause and effect (see Glossary).

Higher guides

Our *higher guides* usually describe themselves as having had many incarnations on the earth plane. Eventually they reach a stage where they no longer need to incarnate in order to further their evolution. They work in groups on the 'other side', and want to communicate with us in order to help us with healing, knowledge, understanding, expansion of vision and our quality of living. Without exception they refer to the imminence of a 'golden age'. They want to help us prepare for that time when the veil between the worlds will be very thin indeed, and the family of humanity will live together in peace and harmony. Without encouraging us to be complacent, the higher guides bring us hope in these difficult and often violent times of change. (See also Bibliography: *A Message of Love*.)

Gildas's identity

All that Gildas has told me about his identity and personal history is that his last incarnation was in the south of France, in the 14th century, as a Benedictine monk. He will probably never incarnate again. Now, his work is teaching and healing. He is one of a group of guides who are seeking to build a bridge of communication between their world and ours, to aid the necessary expansion of vision and concept which is necessary to our transition into the 'golden age'.

The name 'Gildas' means 'a messenger of truth'. Numerous historical references to 14th-century monks called 'Gildas' can be found. Over the years, various readers of our books have brought these to our attention in an attempt to give Gildas, the discarnate communicator, a historical identity. In common with many major communicators from the other side Gildas always resists these attempts to pinpoint him. He explains that, in the realms where guides now have their being, they are no longer limited by past identities and have become more 'diffuse'. Our attempts to give them historical definition could mean that our expectations of them and their teachings would be circumscribed, and thus would colour the questions we ask. Though most guides take on form and personality in order to communicate with us, this is entirely for our benefit as they do not want us to be awe-inspired. The contact they seek with us is one of 'tenderness and loving dialogue'.

Do we all have a personal guide and angel?

There is scientific proof that each time we sleep we all dream dreams. Some people, however, will go through life believing they do not dream, because their dream life is unremembered when they wake.

Similarly, though without the scientific proof, it seems that we all have a guardian angel and at least one guide. Many will go through life unaware of this for several reasons: they may fear, or not believe or be interested in, such phenomena; they may have vague experiences which they are unable to name or categorise; their 'subtle awareness' may be untrained or unawakened; fixed expectations may block the required diffuse awareness.

If you wish to do so, and are willing to let go of various layers of conditioning and fixed expectations, you can learn to sense these beings and to receive or recognise their guidance signs and communications. Not everyone wants to be a 'channel', but most people crave spiritual guidance, a wider perspective on their lives, a sense of meaning and the joy of companionship.

Learning to work with guides and angels means that you will grow less anxious, more hopeful, empowered to bring about personal life changes, and to work towards healing for yourself, humanity and the planet.

Guides will give you wider perspectives, wise counsel and teaching. Angels will help you to tread your path safely, to be involved in the intricate workings of the natural kingdoms, to heal your relationship with nature and to understand the highest principles of existence.

Exercise I
Preparing to Work with Guides and Angels

Make sure that you have some undisturbed time and space, and a notebook, pens and crayons on hand. Play some suitable background music, if you wish.

Light a candle and spend some minutes quietly observing the flame as it burns.

Imagine that this flame is illuminating your life and – taking not more than 15 minutes – write down briefly all the life memories, junctures or feelings which come to you at this moment. Just let them flow in without any striving to remember. When you feel 'stuck', observe the candle flame for a few moments and then continue.

Reflect on what you have remembered or written. What sort of pattern emerges? When you were at crossroads in your life, what factors determined the way you would go? When you were in danger, how were you protected? What are the greatest life lessons you have learned so far?

It might be helpful to share the results of this exercise with a friend or partner. As you consider what has been revealed, look for the times when your life took a new turn or twist. Even though such times may have been difficult consider what you were led towards and what you had to leave behind. Ask yourself whether your guide might have been invisibly at work, keeping you on your true pathway.

Identify the places in life where you resisted change. Try to understand what the resistance was about. Name your hopes, fears and expectations.

Look at the times when you have been in danger, through illness or accident perhaps. Acknowledge the presence of your guardian angel who cannot necessarily prevent mishaps but who *can* make sure that help is at hand.

Reflecting in this way will lay the foundations for acknowledging the guidance and protection in your life. It will help you to work towards a more consciously co-operative relationship with your guides and angels.

2

MOSTLY ABOUT GUIDES

Who or what is my guide? ...Are our guides assigned to us categorically or have we already known them in other lifetimes? ...What determines how my guide appears? ...Why don't I instinctively know my guide? ... Can my grandmother who has just died be my guide? ... Can I have more than one guide? ...Why do most guides seem to be male? ...Are there guides from other planets? ... Exercise 2.

Who or what is my guide?

There are an increasing number of 'channelled' teachings being communicated and published. In addition to those who become fully involved in the channelling scene, many people receive guidance as part of their daily lives and communicate regularly with personal, loving guides who give them comfort and wise counsel.

Gildas has described the being and function of guides:

'The original spark or soul comes from the Source. In order to become *like* the Source and also to ensure that the Source is not static, the soul takes on incarnation and journeys through many lifetimes in search of evolution. Gradually an overseeing, observing or higher self emerges and then each time incarnation takes place only a part of the whole becomes personified in order to undergo the further experience which the essence requires in its search for wholeness.

'When the soul thread is sufficiently evolved, the wheel of rebirth is no longer its main concern or focus. There is then an opportunity to continue on the path of evolution by being of service in different ways. Guides and communicators have agreed to aid the collective journey by sharing the less finite view and wider perspective seen from other planes of being. This is why we seek individuals on earth with whom to communicate. Our aim is to help in making the experience of incarnation less blinkered or limited in vision.

'Guides cross the interface between planes in order to communicate. They have different concerns or aims in making their contact with incarnate human beings. For some, the main focus will be healing, for others teaching, whilst yet others will seek to inspire the artist, poet, architect, musician or writer.

'Even the Great Masters or Ascended Ones seek more direct and constant contact with the earth plane during the times you are now experiencing. You, and therefore we, are at a dangerous but exciting point in the evolution of consciousness.

'Our beings on these planes are more diffuse than are yours on earth. We take on a personality so that we can have more understandable, direct and tender contact with you – but we no longer endure the limitations of personality as you do.

'A great and golden opportunity lies ahead. We communicate in order that in spite of the chaotic or even violent experiences you have, you should not lose hope or faith about the future. We bring positive hope for the potential of humankind to live together in light, love and optimum health.'

Are our guides assigned to us categorically or have we already known them in other lifetimes?

The short answer to this question is that guides are not categorically assigned. The guidance relationship grows throughout evolution, and we will usually have met our guides in previous incarnations. They may already have been dear companions, much loved teachers, healers, priests, priestesses, rulers or leaders.

Yet, since guidance entities are diffuse in their beings, you need to know something of the nature of soul, soul groups, soul families and twin souls in order to understand your basic and previous relationship to your guides.

Gildas describes this aspect of cosmology:

'When a human soul begins its journey it is a spark which splits off from the Source. Choosing human incarnation as its destiny, it partially splits once more. The *yin*, or feminine of its essence, splits from the *yang*, or masculine. These two essences will take different but complementary and interdependent journeys. Each part is like a stem joined at the root or like two strands on a necklace joined at the fastening. Each flower which each stem produces represents an incarnation. The beads on each strand of the necklace represent opportunities for incarnation. Although basically one stem or strand is *yin* and the other *yang*, this does not mean that flowers from the *yin* stem or beads from the *yin* strand will always undergo or choose feminine incarnation, nor will those from the *yang* essence always take on a masculine body – but, at the deepest level, they will carry either a stronger *yin* or stronger *yang* imprint.

Twin souls

'The joined strands or stems are twin souls, essentially sharing an original spark. When evolution is complete, which means that all the beads on the thread have incarnated and returned, the two strands or stems will become one again. During incarnation a flower from one stem or a bead from one strand may meet with a flower or bead from its twin essence, but twin souls do not always incarnate at the same time.

'The complete being does not incarnate. The flowers from the stems or the beads from the threads are aspects of the essential soul. The number of beads on a thread or flowers on a stem varies from soul to soul.

'As well as being twin stems or bead strands, souls belong to families and groups.

Guides

'Your guides will always be from your immediate soul group and probably from your soul family. Usually you will have met each other in the course of incarnation. Occasionally a guide may be your twin soul since it is possible for the evolution of one soul strand to be more accelerated than that of the other.

'Your guide will take on a personality which you are likely to recognise from a previous lifetime.

'Thus, if you have had a happy Native American Indian lifetime in a tribe with a wise chief, your guide may show himself to you in Native American chief's costume, complete with full headdress and eagle's feathers.

'If part of your spiritual journey took place in Atlantis or Tibet your guide may be 'costumed' in such a way as to remind you of past learning and aspirations.

'The guise we wear does not mean that we *are* that person, though that personality is nevertheless incorporated into our essence.

'I chose to appear to Ruth as a Benedictine monk, because my last lifetime, following that rule, in a natural setting in the south of France, was one of gentle contentment and philosophising. Ruth herself

has deep connections to France, so that recognition
between us was easy.

'As our relationship has strengthened, so I am able to
appear in my energy body of light and colour because
Ruth fully recognises and can identify my essence.'

Archetypes

The mode of a guide's appearance is often somewhat arche-
typical. Gildas, in his white Benedictine robe, is also
reminiscent of a hermit or wise old man, with stick and lamp.

A Native American Indian chief, in full regalia complete
with the pipe of peace, embodies the family of humanity in
deep communication with natural laws.

A Tibetan dancer may remind us that life can be a sacred
dance, while a guide with a name such as 'White Flame' will
give us a sense of clarity, eternity and mystery.

In the truly archetypal there is a purity. It is the energy
form which precedes the pseudo-archetype or stereotype. At
one and the same time it embodies the simplicity, yet
complexity, of all great truths.

We live in a society which is confused, rudderless and
lacking true leadership. Guides, with their resonances to
positive, past-life experiences and to the pure archetypes,
bring a sense of continuity, hope, trust, love and abiding
wisdom.

There may be reasons why a discarnate communicator
appears to be harsh, judgemental or manipulative, but all
messages or contacts which are not gentle, loving and
unconditionally supportive in their wisdom should be
severely questioned and challenged. (See Chapter 5.)

Some communicators call themselves such names as: One
of the Disciples; the Virgin Mary; Mary Magdalene; Jesus
or The Direct Voice of God. Such names carry archetypal
energy and represent different aspects of our search for
truth. In guidance we need to seek the highest we can reach.

However, one of the things which must be looked for in

guidance, messages from other worlds and higher beings, is *colouring*. Every communication is, to some extent, coloured by the channel through whom it is spoken. When big claims are made for, or by the communicating guide, we need to be particularly alert to the realisation that 'by their fruits, shall ye know them'. Channelled material can be over-authoritative, incredibly naïve or badly expressed. It is pertinent to ask whether what you are hearing and perhaps intending to act upon, is congruent with the source from which it is claimed to come. (See also Chapter 5.)

Earlier I used the term 'higher guides'. This means that there are also low level entities from other dimensions who can, and do, masquerade as guides and may give gullible channels and listeners an imposing name in order to gain attention.

Equally, there are people channelling who have not cleared their own psychological material sufficiently and who may colour the name of their source because of a need themselves to be seen as important or specially chosen.

What determines how my guide appears?

Guides want you to feel comfortable and at ease with them. They will usually appear in a form or mode which is acceptable and attractive to you. The guise they choose may help you to connect with pleasant memories from a previous life-time, or may conform, to some extent, to your expectations of how a guide *should* appear. Guides do not necessarily emerge as a particular character, but give a sense of their presence or come to you in their energy bodies of light, colour and fragrance.

Why don't I instinctively know my guide?

If you had awareness of your guides as a matter of course probably you would never learn to make your own choices and decisions or to live your own life. It is a spiritual paradox that guides usually communicate with you most clearly when you have reached that stage of life and development where you are happy to make your own decisions. Guides are not there to live your life for you or to save you from the results of your actions. A friend recently remarked to me: 'I know why I cannot contact my guide clearly. If I could, I would be bothering him the whole time for theories and explanations and I just wouldn't get on with living.'

Can my grandmother, who has just died, be my guide?

Your true guides are highly evolved beings. It is perfectly possible that your grandmother or other relations may have been part of a very evolved soul stem or thread and so can become a guide for you after their death. Yet this is rare. Mostly, after death, there is much personal work and healing to be done before the choices of where to continue work and evolution are made.

Sometimes, you may find a loved one is very close to you immediately after death to help you through your grief and in overcoming any difficulties you may be experiencing.

It is also important to realise that departure from the physical body does not necessarily confer wisdom. Some mediums specialise in bringing messages from dead relatives or friends. Before we rush to take advice from 'Uncle Fred' we should ask ourselves whether the mere fact of his death has made his views any more valuable than those we might have hesitated to listen to six months previously when he was still alive. A fool during life may be equally foolish in the hereafter.

Can I have more than one guide?

Once you become aware of guides, it is likely that you will meet more than one who has special wisdom for you. Some people become aware that their guide is the 'spokesperson' for a group of guides. Without special training it is unwise just to be open to any discarnate entity who wishes to make contact. For channelling purposes it is better to try to develop a connection with one particular guide so that confidence can build and authenticity be assured. (See Chapter 5 for more on this.)

Why do most guides seem to be male?

It is true that the majority of guides do seem to appear in the masculine gender. It is equally true that there are a number of female guides who communicate regularly. Since an evolved being is beyond gender it seems that if your guide's intention is to give teachings he will appear as masculine. Teaching demands use of the masculine, rather than the feminine principle. Healing and comforting guides may be feminine, because these activities depend more on feminine, rather than masculine principles.

It is also true that however many changes are being brought about in the balance of power between men and women, the world is still very biased towards the masculine when it comes to authority. Guides who want to be heard may therefore choose the masculine gender. This is a collusion which needs to be broken and guides should be aware of this. Recently Gildas declined to answer a question in depth, saying 'a feminine guide could give more profound teaching on this matter'. Perhaps, even among guides, things are beginning to change.

Are there guides from other planets?

There are a number of channels who regularly receive messages from guides who identify themselves as coming from other planets or even from other galaxies. Contact made in this way may be one of the answers to learning how to overcome the barriers of time and space which so far limit space travel, and our ability to discover and communicate with other intelligences in the universe.

Exercise 2
Finding the Place of Inner Peace and Wisdom

This is a second preparatory exercise for guidance. If you practise it regularly it will mean that you can more easily hear your inner guidance and that if you wish to have contact with discarnate guides and angels you will be meeting them from your true, wise, self.

Make sure that you will be undisturbed. Create a quiet space for yourself and lie or sit comfortably in a position in which your body is symmetrically arranged.

Be in touch with the rhythm of your breathing. Do not try to alter or force it; just follow each in-breath and each out-breath until you begin to feel centred, calm and peaceful.

Now visualise your heart chakra (in the centre of your body near your physical heart), opening up like a rose in perfect bloom ... Imagine that you are travelling to the golden centre of this rose ... In this golden centre, which is the focus point of your being, there is a still point of wisdom and knowing ... Remain there, quietly, for up to ten minutes, knowing that when you return you will have gained a new perspective on any pressing problems which are besetting you in your outer life.

When you are ready, return to an awareness of your breath rhythm ... Let the petals of your heart centre gently close in ... Feel your contact with the ground beneath your feet ... Take your sense of peace with you as you resume your normal life once more.

3

YE HOLY ANGELS BRIGHT

> The angelic hierarchy ... Divine principles and arche-
> types of higher qualities ... The winged hosts ...
> Lucifer – the fallen angel ... Invocation ... Exercises
> 3 and 4.

The angelic hierarchy

Belief in angels is woven into the fabric of humanity's spiritual search. From untutored reverence through to myths,
tribal belief systems and every form of religious practice,
angels have been recipients of prayer as well as guests at
celebrations and rituals.

In the Christian religion the presence and acknowledgement of angels has brought a welcome lightness, modifying
the heavy morality and the concept of a patriarchal, anthro-
pomorphic, judgemental god.

Angels are indeed holy and bright. They bring us light
and laughter, as well as enabling our finite minds to arrive
at a wider understanding of divinity, infinity and the scheme
of the universe.

The main esoteric teachings about angels come from
Zoroastrian (see Glossary) and Hebraic sources. In this
chapter, the information offered about the angelic hierar-
chies is taken from a number of different sources and
presented in a 'scheme' which Gildas suggests as being
workable.

Many discarnate guides are now suggesting that angels are seeking a more personal relationship with humans. They are eager to teach us about the nature of light and to help us understand the dimension of levity as well as that of gravity.

Guides are part of the human stream of consciousness but angels are not. Guides have been incarnate. Angels will never be incarnate. Guides and humans will never be angels.

Angels belong to a collective body, within which there is mutual support and an evolutionary pattern. They emanate from the Divine Source and are divided into groups. Each group has a specific task or area of interest.

Divine principles and archetypes of higher qualities

The multiple facets of the divine impulse or mind which governs the universe are mirrored to us by the different groups of angels. Spiritual philosophies speak of divine principles. Transpersonal psychologists such as Ferrucci (see Bibliography) refer to 'archetypes of higher qualities', in a common attempt to describe some of the great ideals, impulses and aspirations experienced by human beings.

A divine principle or archetype of higher quality exists first of all as an abstract *energy* which develops into a named concept. Peace, Beauty, Wholeness, Justice, Love, Order, Health, Creation, Harmony and Balance are among the concepts which fall into this category.

These energies constitute the angelic essence. When you seek to fulfil the potentials of human living you are dealing with angelic substance. You can feel more supported in personal and collective growth if you name the angels you wish to aid or bless you and consciously invoke their help and support. The word 'angel' means messenger. When interacting with angels you can send messages into the cosmos as well as receiving them – the messenger service is two-way.

The winged hosts

Fairies, elementals, nature spirits and devas (see Glossary) are part of the same energy stream as angels. There is an evolutionary progression from the life-force which helps plants and minerals to grow through to angels, archangels and the higher ranks of the heavenly hosts.

There are three main angelic realms and each realm has three sub-divisions. The angels which are said to be closest to the divine energy are called Heavenly Counsellors. Their sub-divisions are as follows.

Seraphim

Seraphim are the most highly evolved angels who work to keep the right balance, alignment and movement between planets, stars and other heavenly bodies by working with sound or conducting the music of the spheres.

Cherubim

Cherubim are the true light workers in that they work as guardians of all the light and colour energy in the universe. They help to direct and transform the light which streams from the sun, moon and stars, so that it can be received in those places where it is most needed. They help to maintain the bridge of light between the planes of higher and lower vibration.

Earth is a plane of lower vibration. Our bodies are the protective clothing we need in order to function on the earth plane. Our souls and spirits have higher vibrational rates but direct, divine light is too intense for our bodies to sustain. The bridge of light means that we can safely have higher vision and extra-sensory or mystical experience. Guides and angels cross the bridge of light in order to meet us more closely. Spiritual training practices such as meditation and the channelling of healing help to strengthen our energy bodies so that we can also meet the higher beings on the bridge in order to have clearer and safer contact with them (see pages 38–9 for more on this).

Thrones

Thrones are the angelic overseers of each planet. The throne angel who oversees the earth works in co-operation with the seraphim to keep it on course and in right relationship to the other planets. The earth throne also concerns itself with balances between species and endeavours to prevent or modify such cataclysmic disasters as major floodings, volcanic eruptions, widespread drought or earthquakes. Each planet has its own throne.

The next angelic realm is that of Heavenly Governors. The sub-divisions are as follows.

Dominions

Dominions are the counsellors, advisers, supporters and teachers of all evolving angels. They particularly assist each guardian angel in looking after the well being of the incarnate individual to whom they have been assigned.

Virtues

Virtues are the listeners, who respond to prayers and requests for healing by directing appropriate concentrations of divine energy into specific areas or towards particular individuals.

Powers

Powers are the inspirers of human consciousness or higher ideals who also oversee the rhythms of birth, death and rebirth.

Spiritual teachings often refer to the 'akashic records', Jung wrote extensively about 'the collective unconscious' and Rupert Sheldrake speaks of 'morphic resonance'. These are different ways of expressing the belief that every human thought and action creates waves which affect all other members of the human race, as well as being subtly recorded in the collective memory bank. Reincarnationists believe that there are personal as well as collective akashic records. The personal version records each soul's evolutionary journey. The collective version holds the imprint of all human experience and learning.

The powers are keepers of the akashic records, guardians of the collective unconscious and instigators of morphic resonance.

The third angelic realm is the Messengers. The sub-divisions are as follows.

Principalities

Principalities are the overseers and guardians of large groups and organisations, nations and cities.

Archangels

Archangels overlight all aspects of human endeavour and help us to name, interpret and work with, divine principles or the archetypes of higher qualities. The most commonly named and those dealt with in this book are Michael, Gabriel, Uriel and Raphael.

Archangels can be invoked to bring blessing, safety and protection into our daily lives, and to assist us in gaining greater clarity about our life's purposes.

Angels without other titles

Those who come closest to our earthly vibrations and bring us angelic qualities such as joy, laughter, harmony, peace, love, synchronicity – and many others.

Included in this sub-division are our Guardian Angels.

Each time the soul decides to embark on the process of incarnation a guardian angel comes into being through the process of evolution from nature spirits and devas (see Glossary). Therefore from before gestation to the journey into and beyond death each one of us is accompanied by an angelic presence, who without interfering with our freedom of choice will lovingly guide and protect us. When we die, our guardian angels guide us through that great journey and only when we have completely adapted to life beyond the body do they move on to the next stage of their evolution or to another task within the angelic hierarchy.

(It is usual to speak of angels as 'he'. Many have names traditionally given to men and boys. Women often find this masculine orientation difficult to accept. When necessary I use the traditional 'he' to avoid clumsiness of style. Angels are beyond gender and fully balanced in masculine and feminine principle. Like humans, some use more of the masculine principle for their work and some more of the feminine.)

Mainly it is the archangels who are given traditional and specific names.

Michael means 'Who is like the Divine'. He is guardian of the direction of the north, of night-time, of the season of winter, of the element of air, spirits and dreams. His special colour is blue.

Michael brings the blessings of co-operation, reconciliation and peace. He encourages us to live in harmony with others and with the earth. He teaches us to ask the right questions at the right time.

Gabriel means 'The Divine is my strength'. He is the guardian of the south, noon, summer and our emotions. His element is water and his colour is green.

Gabriel is the angel of revelation and hope. It was he who told Mary she was pregnant with Jesus. He especially blesses and protects women and children, and may be invoked to bring healing to dysfunctional families.

(Including perhaps the largest, most dysfunctional family: that of humanity as a whole.)

Uriel means 'The light and fire of the Divine'. He is the guardian of the east, the rising sun, dawn, morning and spring. His element is fire and his colour yellow.

Uriel blesses our minds and inspires the worlds of science, economics, politics, political reform and medical research. He is connected with spiritual alchemy.

Uriel urges us towards social equality and helps us to find our direction in life.

Raphael means 'The Divine has healed'. He is the guardian of the west, twilight, evening, autumn and healing. His element is earth and his colour is red. He blesses growth, transformation and all forms of healing, from surgery to herbalism, and the 'laying on of hands'. He brings comfort and protection to all who are physically, spiritually or emotionally ill.

The fallen angel

Lucifer is the angel who, in the traditional myths, was expelled from the hierarchy because he wanted too much power. He is often thought of as being seductive and evil, yet his name means 'light'.

There is a parallel between the myth of Lucifer, and that of the expulsion of Adam and Eve from Paradise because of their eating of the fruit of the tree of knowledge.

Another perspective on Lucifer is to see him not as a bringer of evil, but as the closest companion to the human journey. If we see the choice to seek knowledge and experience not as a 'fall' but as an evolutionary journey, then we may see Lucifer as the angelic being who made an important sacrifice in order to journey with us. His light enables us to see the darker side of things, by casting the shadow from which we learn the lessons of evolution. He endeavours to communicate the conditions of earth to the other angels and to the Divine Source so that they can all better assist us in dealing with those conditions.

The potential for working with angels

One of the questions most frequently asked by spiritually seeking people is 'How can we help our world spiritually and energetically as well as practically?' The assembly of angels offers an abundance of ways in which to meditate, pray, send out the light, work towards self-knowledge and expand your thought processes.

A good way for you to begin working with angels is to get to know the powers and joys of invocation.

The dictionary definition of 'invocation' is comprehensive.

> The act or the form of invoking or addressing in prayer or supplication; an appellation under which one is invoked; any formal invoking of the blessing or help of a god or saint, etc.; an opening prayer in a public religious service or in the Litany; a call for inspiration from a Muse or other deity as at the beginning of a poem; an incantation or calling up of a spirit; a call or summons.

An invocation gains power when it is spoken aloud with as much confidence as possible. It is a call for inspiration, naming the name of the one you choose to be your inspirer. It focuses the mind and the intention, and makes a bridge of awareness. It helps to strengthen your awareness and to increase your subtle energetic strengths.

Begin your work with angels by carrying out this invocation exercise.

Exercise 3
Making an Invocation to an Angel

Begin by rereading the list of angels and their purposes in this chapter. As you do so reflect on your life and your needs. At this moment, what quality would you like to have more present in your life or which worries would you like eased? Which kind of angel do you feel will most help you to draw this quality towards you?

Here are some suggestions to help you choose.

- If you would like to be more aware of the spiritual worlds and the patterns of the universe you need the help of *the seraphim*.
- If you would like to feel a greater sense of Communion with the Divine you need *the cherubim*.
- If you are plagued by fears of natural disasters you need *the thrones*.
- If you feel you may have been giving your guardian angel a bad time lately, you need *the dominions* to give your guardian angel support and so help to strengthen the contact between you.
- If you wish to send light or prayer to someone or some situation, or if you doubt that your prayers are ever heard you need *the virtues*.
- If you feel that whatever you do to help others or the universe is a small insignificant drop in the ocean; if you are expecting a birth or death in the family you need *the powers*.
- If you want to feel more in touch with your national heritage, or to bless the city in which you live or a particular large group to which you belong, you need *the principalities*.
- If you want peace or reconciliation or to work more with your dreams you need *the Archangel Michael*.
- If you need family healing, more hopefulness or a sense of protection you need *the Archangel Gabriel*.
- If you need help in finding direction in your life; if you suffer from an illness for which, as yet, there is little medical help; if you have money worries, need clarity of mind or are concerned

about social reform you could work with *the Archangel Uriel*.
- If you are discontented with normality and find life static or tedious; need to feel more grounded; need physical, emotional, mental or spiritual healing, you could work with *the Archangel Raphael*.
- If you want to bring a particular angelic quality such as joy, delight, love, willingness, beauty or harmony more consciously into your life, then you need the angel who carries that quality: the angel of joy; the angel of delight; the angel of love; the angel of willingness etc.

If you want to feel closer to your guardian angel then use this invocation to help. Then try the exercise which follows this one.

When you have selected the angel you would like to invoke, spend a few moments thinking about the wording of your invocation. It is important to name the angel or its sub-division, so you might begin:

- Archangel Michael who blesses our dreams ... ; or
- I invoke, from the ranks of the heavenly governors one of the angels known as 'virtues' ... ; or
- I invoke the angel of beauty ...

After these initial words you will need to write down others which clarify the nature of the help you wish to invoke. Keep the invocation fairly short. You need enough words, but simplicity, clarity and dignity are even more vital.

When you have written your invocation, practise reading it aloud and make any alterations needed. When you are ready to use it prepare yourself by lighting a candle, sounding a bell or having some inspirational objects such as crystals near you. Take up a balanced body position, stretch your arms to the heavens and, if possible, say your invocation aloud, three times, in a strong voice.

If it is not possible to speak aloud, go through each word clearly, but silently, also three times.

When you have finished, expect the angel of your choice to

manifest its presence in numerous large and small ways. You will probably notice coincidences or feel a new kind of awareness. You may sense flashes of angelic light or the brush of angel wings. You may dream a specially meaningful dream or find a creative solution to a problem. The signs that your invocation has been heard will be there if you watch for them with an open expectation.

Exercise 4
Drawing your Guardian Angel Closer to You

Sit or lie in a comfortable but symmetrically balanced position, making sure that you will be undisturbed. Have ready a blanket for warmth, and crayons and paper for any drawing or writing which you may wish to do to record your experience.

Be aware of the rhythm of your breathing ... Gradually bring that rhythm into your heart centre or chakra (see Glossary) ... Travel on the heart energy into your inner landscape ... Find yourself in a meadow ... Awaken your inner senses, so that you see the objects and colours around you ... Hear the sounds ... Smell the fragrances ... Touch the textures ... Taste the tastes ...

In your meadow there is a rainbow ... In the inner world, unlike the outer, you can actually see and experience the rainbow's beginning or ending ... All the brilliant, translucent colours of the spectrum are pouring down onto the earth ... Go and stand in this rainbow of light ... As you experience the colours ask that the particular colour which will help you and your guardian angel to draw closer may flood into you, and bring you healing and harmony ...

Leave the rainbow, but as you walk out into the meadow once more the colour of your choice – or the one which was chosen you – will continue to surround you ... Feel yourself beginning to soften a little at the edges and merge into the colour ...

Let the colour become soft in texture around you, like the gentle brushing and protection of an angel's wings ... Feel lightened and protected, but also free as the colour becomes your guardian angel, gently holding you ...

Your angel may have more than one colour in its light ... Let these develop and feel their protective quality ...

Remember a time in your life when you really felt that although you were in danger, or at risk, there was a protective influence with you ... Thank your guardian angel for that intervention ... Ask your guardian angel to make you more and more conscious of the protection and help which is with you at all times ...

When you are ready to return to the outer world, make your journey through the meadow with the sense of your angel behind you, or at your side ... Return to an awareness of the rhythm of your breathing in your heart centre ... Become aware of your physical body and particularly of your contact with the ground ... Bring the sense of your guardian angel's presence and colours right through into your outer world ... Remember those colours and the strong, but gentle presence of your guardian angel whenever you feel anxious or in need.

It is good to repeat this exercise weekly if possible. It also helps to try to have some of the colours which you experienced in the meadow or as belonging to your guardian angel in your everyday environment. Crystals, coloured glass bottles or silk scarves often carry the right colour quality.

4

MOSTLY ABOUT ANGELS

What do angels and fairies look like? ...What is the progression from fairies and nature spirits to angelic beings? ...Will my guardian angel always be with me? ... If there is an earth angel why are there earth-quakes and other natural disasters? ... Did Hitler have a guardian angel? ... Could I be protected, even from death, by the presence of my guardian angel? ... How can I help my children to stay closer to the other worlds? ... How can I overcome my fear of altered states of consciousness, other planes and the beings who inhabit them? ... Exercises 5, 6 and 7.

What do angels and fairies look like?

The simple answer is that angels look like angels just as fairies look like fairies. The traditional representations we have all seen express a universal truth. Perhaps many illustrators of angels and fairies have had developed psychic vision, while others have merely followed the known and therefore universally recognisable.

At the highest level, angels, fairies and guides are pure energy, and therefore we tend to recognise their presence by feeling, sensation or a subtle 'knowing'. On the occasions when we glimpse them more physically they are bright beings, manifesting in a movement of light, a sense of surreal shimmering, flashes or patterns of brilliant colour.

When we see them in the most physical manifestation of which they are capable then, in order to aid our perception, they take on echoes of the form which we most associate with being or individuality – the human form. They organise their energies in such a way as to be recognisable, but they do not intrinsically carry that shape. For example, the answer to the question 'Do angels have feet' is 'Not usually'. They do not need them as they are not bound to the ground by gravity, as we are.

The wings which are associated with fairies and angels indicate their ability to move swiftly, to hover into our field of vision and out again, and are our sense of the energy trail which they have. Angelic wings have rather more substance than fairy wings and, particularly with our guardian angels, it is possible to get a physically tangible sense of their softness and protection as they enfold us.

What is the progression from fairies and nature spirits to angelic beings?

The stream from the Divine Source, of which elementals, fairies, nature spirits and devas are a part, has a simpler model of evolution than does the human stream. Humans have chosen the path of knowledge, experience and individuation which is usually meandering and tortuous. The angelic stream is one of energetic manifestation and progressive higher awareness, with fewer opportunities for individual choice and without emphasis on individuation.

Elementals are the lowest manifestation within the angelic hierarchy. They are tiny energy beings generally associated with plants, trees, the natural environment and the elements. When seen by humans, they may appear as tiny points of light or colour, or in traditional fairy form, as nereids, sylphs, undines, salamanders, gnomes, elves or flower fairies.

Devas evolve from the elementals and flower fairies. The word 'deva' is from Sanskrit and means 'good shining spirit'. They often become very tall and their task is one of guardianship of large trees, forests, rivers and watercourses, the movement of air, balance of climate, the interchange of the seasons, fertility, seedtime and harvest. Sometimes they guard buildings, holy shrines or places where there is a particularly sacred energy within the earth. The devic beings' next step in evolution is to become angels – probably beginning as a guardian angel accompanying a human being throughout an earth incarnation.

Will my guardian angel always be with me?

Your guardian angel will always be with you throughout your present lifetime. This accompanying presence came into being at the moment at which your soul decided you would incarnate and was there at your conception, throughout your gestation and at your birth. Your guardian angel will be with you at your death and will accompany you through that transition until you are at peace in the realms of light. He will then move on to his next stage of evolution.

The same guardian angel will not be with you through every incarnation. Each time you incarnate a new guardian angel takes over your guidance.

If there is an earth angel why are there earthquakes, floods, volcanic eruptions and other natural disasters?

Humanity has a symbiotic relationship with the earth. When the family of humanity is dysfunctional, then the earth also becomes dysfunctional. Just as our physical bodies rid themselves of toxins through such diseases as colds and flu, so the earth rids herself of the pollutions and misuses humankind has imposed upon her. Angels will endeavour to bring healing and to maintain natural balances, but they do not directly interfere with our free will. Where that free will impinges upon the earth we must expect there to be consequences and reactions.

The earth is also evolving. Some natural disturbances are part of her change and growth. Perhaps if we were more in tune with earth and her angels her natural eruptions would not have assumed such disastrous or cataclysmic proportions. The things we have created and the ways in which we have placed them would have been harmonious with natural laws or, in the words of a prayer given by Gildas, 'more truly in the Divine image'.

Did Hitler have a guardian angel? If so, why didn't the angel prevent him from doing the dreadful things he did?

Everyone has a guardian angel – even Hitler – but it is not the angel's task to live our lives for us. Angels and guides will try to make themselves heard but if we are determined on a certain course, they cannot override us. Only when we are in co-operation with them or with natural forces of harmony, can they steer us to live our lives to the fullest positive potential.

When human beings tread a dark or destructive path, they have cut themselves off from the light, which always lies just beyond the self-made or self-inflicted darkness.

We must be careful not to opt out of responsibility for our actions and those of our fellow beings. We must never take an over-simplistic view. It is often the experience of either personal or collective darkness which proves to be the greatest catalyst. We all wish that holocausts, wars and oppression could never happen – when we become fully conscious of our joint responsibilities and choices in these matters, they never will. Evil will only be ousted when we choose to let it go, not by Divine intervention. We cannot have free choice *and* complete protection or rescue from the results of our own actions.

Could I be protected, even from death, by the presence of my guardian angel?

Our lives have their natural and appointed rhythm, from the moment of birth to the moment of death. Part of the guardianship which our angels undertake is connected with that rhythm. They will therefore endeavour to guard us from premature death by intervening in our follies or aiding our healing processes. There are circumstances, such as death by suicide, when we wilfully interfere with our allotted life span, but otherwise our angels will be particularly present at moments when unscheduled death might happen.

How can I help my children to stay closer to the other worlds?

Many children have a natural resonance to fairies, angels, guides and the things of the spirit. Most learn, from an early age, not to speak of these things and, in order to conform to the norm, also learn how to shut them out.

Children who stay sensitive to subtle perceptions are those who receive attentive listening when they share their experiences, who see adult respect for nature, beauty and harmony, and who are not made to feel that 'childish things' are of little importance.

Children can be taught to relax into quiet contemplation and encouraged to maintain a sense of wonder. So many adults have lost touch with their inner 'golden child' and consequently with the art of delight or joy. To help your outer children to maintain what you have lost you must be prepared to relearn and revive a fresh approach to life.

Many parents clamp down on the things children say or report, because they are afraid that, as school time comes up, there will be teasing from peers, already conditioned to shallow over-conformity and defence of the status quo.

It is perfectly possible to make quite a young child understand that some things can be said at home and not at school. Eventually we all have to learn that in our complex world there are a number of masks we are obliged to wear. The danger comes when we identify with a particular mask and lose touch with passion and vulnerability.

Children understand far more than we give them credit for. If you want your child to remain sensitive never under-rate the child, never 'talk down' and never over-protect.

How can I overcome my fears of altered states of consciousness, other planes and the beings who inhabit them?

Fears are often healthy defences and should be respected so that what we are *actually* afraid of can be defined.

Often there are fears of going mad, getting lost in another world – unable to return, being taken over or possessed or becoming a freak in the eyes of our friends (see page 2).

Working with guides and angels is a supportive way of learning about other worlds and how to negotiate safely the pathways between them, but it cannot be repeated too often that the work of self-knowledge and strengthening should not only go alongside spiritual exploration but also be seen as an integral part of it.

Working with changes of consciousness needs skilful guidance. Protective measures are simple but vital. Instructions like 'make sure that you will be undisturbed' are there to help you protect against being jolted too quickly from inner to outer activity. Setting time boundaries for the work puts it in proportion in your life. Making sure your feet are on the ground at the end of a journey and taking time to adjust to your outer environment helps you to travel fully from one activity to another. Visualising light around you is not a shielding device, but a means of strengthening your energy body. Once you are surrounded in light, you take it with you both as a protection for your-self and a gift to the environment.

If you are joining a spiritual group try to make sure that

there are fun-loving, thoroughly earthed people in it who are leading whole and successful lives. Beware of those who see spiritual development as some kind of elated 'trip' or as an excuse for being 'way out'.

With simple measures which honour the natural steps of development, no one gets lost in other worlds or meditational space, never to return. As you work through this book, remember that every instruction and the sequence of the work has been carefully thought out. If you are in doubt, seek advice. Before you undertake a course of work alone, make sure that you know where support will be available, if necessary. Counsellors trained in transpersonal perspectives or psychosynthesis and reliably known healers will be ready to help and reassure.

Taking events one step at a time will melt your fears. Trying to ignore or override them will tend to make them increase rather than dissipate. Don't immediately discuss what you are doing with over-sceptical friends. Before long they will probably be asking what is making you so much more self-assured and giving you confidence.

Exercise 5
Aura Strengthening

For this exercise it is best to stand up. If you need to sit or lie, then make sure that your body is as straight and symmetrically aligned as possible.

Be in touch with the rhythm of your breathing and gradually let that rhythm touch your heart centre (see Glossary), so that you know that each breath you breathe is activating your heart energy.

Imagine your energy field (aura) all around you like an egg of light surrounding and emanating from your physical body ... It encompasses you, so that you are at its centre ... Because it is energy it interpenetrates with matter, so it continues into the earth beneath your feet and is not impeded by bed, chair or ground if you are sitting or lying ...

Experiment with expanding and contracting your egg of light ... Bring it in close to you ... Push it right out from you into the room by making the egg larger or thicker so that you remain closely surrounded by light which interacts with your physical body ...

Finish this experimentation by drawing your aura in again ... Feel at ease in your energy field ...

Check your body posture ... Your feet should be comfortably apart, your knees bent, your joints loose, your shoulders down and your head well balanced on your neck ...

Your aura is the centre of your sacred, psychic temple ... It is contained within an inner sanctuary and beyond that are two courtyards, an inner and an outer ... Between each area of the temple there is a door ... Be aware that you are the doorkeeper ... You decide who enters your temple, and into which areas you invite them ...

Be aware of the quality of energy you would wish to be within your inner sanctuary ... Be aware of the quality of energy which would be invasive to your sacred temple ... Determine to be more aware of your responsibility for guardianship ...

Keeping the awareness of your temple around you, be conscious of your contact with the ground and of your everyday surroundings ... When you are ready return to your everyday activities.

Try to remember your temple often during the course of your normal day, so that you become more aware of your ability to keep a distance or to invite people to be close, and so that you are less vulnerable to invasion by other people's energies.

Exercise 6
Connecting the Higher Self to the Lower Self
(Higher Will to Lower Will)

Stand or sit with your back as straight but also as comfortable as possible ... Lean against something for support if you need to ... Balance your head on your neck, so that you get a feeling of bodily alignment ... Be aware of your solar plexus area or chakra (see

Glossary) ... Also be aware of your crown chakra and a point just above it ...

The point just above your crown chakra represents the point of contact with your higher self ... Imagine a stream of pure golden light coming from your higher self, through your crown chakra, through the centre of your body, interpenetrating with your physical substance and into the centre of your solar plexus ... Hold the golden light in your solar plexus and then breathe it out into and beyond your auric space ...

Breathe golden light down from the higher self point on each in-breath ... Hold it in the centre of your solar plexus for a count of three ... Breathe it out firmly through the solar plexus and your auric space on each out-breath ...

Continue to do this for about ten breath sequences ...

Be aware of your contact with the earth and feel your normal breath rhythm as you return to your everyday tasks.

Exercise 7
Establishing an Inner Meeting Place for Work with Guides and Angels

First turn back to Exercise 2 on inner widsom to refresh your memory.

Sit or lie in a comfortable but symmetrically balanced position, making sure that you will be undisturbed. Have ready a blanket for warmth, and crayons and paper for any recording you may wish to do.

Be aware of the rhythm of your breathing ... Gradually bring that rhythm into your heart centre or chakra and recreate your place of inner wisdom ...

Travel on the heart and wisdom energy into your inner landscape and find yourself in a meadow ... Activate all your inner senses so that you see the objects and colours ... Smell the fragrances ... Hear the sounds ... Touch the textures ... Savour the tastes ...

From your meadow look out at the surrounding landscape ...

Quite nearby there is a winding pathway which leads into hills and continues up into some mountains ...

You are going to take this pathway, knowing that you are going to a plateau which is near the top of one of the mountains, but not beyond the tree line ...

Make your way to the plateau in your own time, noting the scenery through which you pass as you go ...

At the plateau take time to explore ... You will probably find a source of clear running water from which to refresh yourself and there may be a small sanctuary or travellers' rest ... There may be a place of natural sanctuary with a sun-warmed rock against which to rest your back and look out over the landscape ... As you explore the plateau you are looking for a place where you are happy to sit and wait, with an open heart and an open expectation ...

When you have settled yourself in the place of your choice, enjoy the peace ... If there is a question in your heart, hold it there, pondering it in a relaxed way ...

At this stage do not expect or invite a presence to be with you, but spend the time establishing this as a meeting place ... You have made your part of the journey ... This territory is yours but be aware that it is also part of the bridge to other worlds ...

Stay here for not more than ten minutes ... When you are ready to return, drink again from the water source ... Make your way back to the meadow ...

From the meadow return to the awareness of your breath in your heart centre ... To the awareness of your body and your contact with the ground ... To your outer surroundings ... Visualise a cloak of light with a hood, right around you ...

Take time to record your journey in words or drawing ...

Return to your everyday routines.

5

CLEARING THE WAY FOR GUIDANCE

From Pisces to Aquarius ... The phenomenon of colouring ... Vocabulary ... Authority issues and conditioning ... Sub-personalities ... Expectations and mind set ... Models ... Ways in which guidance manifests ... Exercises 8 and 9.

From Pisces to Aquarius

We are moving into a new millenium. We expect change. The year 2000 also means that astrologically we are moving into the influence of a new sign, something which happens, at a collective level, only once every 2000 years. We are leaving the Age of Pisces to arrive in the Age of Aquarius. We cannot escape change.

The point at which one sign changes to another is known as 'the cusp'. In the normal astrological year, the cusp may last for a day or so, but in the great, 2000 year cycles, it is proportionately longer. Although we are several years from the celebrations for the millennium, the influence of the sign of Aquarius is already active.

The cuspal point, as the retreating influence gives way to the one which is emerging, can be tricky. Uncertainties, insecurities and the breakdown of old systems are to be expected. Even favourable change and the positive opportunities which will emerge can be unsettling and demand-ing. The retreat of Pisces and the emergence of Aquarius are currently presenting challenges to humanity and the planet. Particularly affected by this change in astrological influence are the fields of mediumship, channelling and spiritual phenomena.

Pisces is a water sign. Its glyph or symbol shows two fish swimming in opposite directions to form a circle. Spiritually, Pisces makes us flow towards the saviour, guru, teacher or parent/redeemer. It leads us to understand the nature of sacrifice but tends to fix us in the role of disciple, devotee, pupil or spiritual child. Though it inspires the collective search for spiritual truth it also leads us into the dogmatic jungle. At an individual level it fosters depen-dency and a slavish obedience to authority.

Aquarius, an air sign, despite its glyph or symbol of the water carrier, urges us to individuality and encourages the finding of our own *inner* wisdom and authority. It makes us question outer authority and known patterns with a healthy cynicism. In the first flush of its influence, as we realise more fully the need for self-development and self-responsibility, it will tend to make for difficulties in community life, families, partnerships and all joint ventures. As the phase of assertion comes to an end we will become more mutually tolerant and respectful, honouring and valuing each others' differences. This will enable the development of spiritually and emotionally mature rela-tionships, systems of government and community dynamics.

How do these changes affect the guidance scene? The Piscean medium could often be a passive channel with little required other than a natural gift for openness to other worlds and the beings who inhabit them. The Age of Pisces is the age of the full trance medium, often allowing another entity to enter completely and take over the physical body for a prescribed period of time. It is the age of psychic phenomena when many marvels undoubtedly happened, but deliberate fraudulent fakings were also exposed.

The Aquarian model of relating to other worlds and entities opens new perspectives and brings new challenges. The
new channel will rarely enter full trance – a lightly altered
state of consciousness being sufficient. Dramatic phenomena will no longer be sought. It will be easy to be
self-deluding but where drama is less to the fore, deliberate
fraud will be largely a thing of the past. The main dilemma
for the Aquarian channel and those who seek discarnate
guidance is the phenomenon of colouring.

The phenomenon of colouring

Within every field of endeavour a certain jargon is bound
to develop. Colouring covers a number of implications of
which you should be well aware before going to consult a
guide through a channel/medium, reading channelled information or attempting to become a channel yourself.

Consciousness of colouring will prevent you from giving
the contents of channelled messages too much authority
without due consideration; alert you to the need for interpretation; and make you more thoughtful about the nature
of your guides and the processes of channelling and guidance.

The Aquarian model of guidance is one of co-operation
between guides, angels and incarnate individuals. It is about
dialogue and a more conscious form of mediumship.

Without full trance the channel's own belief systems,
authority hang-ups, limitations in vocabulary, imperfect
attunement or emotional attachment to the results can all
colour and affect the messages received. Yet continuing full
trance mediumship is out of the question. The coming
changes require a conscious co-operation between the
worlds, even – or perhaps especially – though this also tends
to throw us back on ourselves and makes us face our many-
faceted inadequacies.

In the new channelling we will only hear what we are
capable of hearing, and unless we work to clear ourselves

of conditioning and hang-ups – particularly around authority – we will perpetuate the saviour/disciple, guru/devotee,
teacher/pupil and parent/redeemer/child archetypes well
beyond their sell-by dates.

As we work towards guidance, not only will our guides
help us to know ourselves, but the process of achieving
clear connections and messages of value will require self-
searching.

Many people who have started to receive messages from
their guides complain that it is difficult to get clear guidance for themselves and those very close to them. Of course
it is!

When I attune to Gildas to get his comments on the problems of those who come to consult us, I know that I can
stay detached from what the answers may be. The dilemmas which come into my work-room move me, activate my
compassion, have me open-mouthed at the courageous
ways in which people manage their lives and the burdens
they have to bear, but I don't have difficulty in getting
myself out of the way so that Gildas's perspective on the
questions asked can be clearly channelled.

When it comes to asking for myself, if I hear what I want
to hear I suspect that I may have coloured the responses. I
also always fear that when channelling for close and loved
ones, what *I* want for them may slip through. Before asking
Gildas for advice for them I have to work hard at making
conscious any emotional investment I may have.

Guides have their own particular characteristics.
Especially when working with a channel, they show interesting personalities. However if you receive guidance from
a guide who appears to have an 'axe to grind', take a close
look at the channel. Do they have too much reverence for
authority? Or too little? Do they have a tendency to be
judgemental? Are they too conservative or too liberal? Do
they sit on the fence and fear commitment? Are they
capable of clear, detached thinking? If guides have tendencies which echo any extremism in the channel, colouring is
probably present. Since none of us can ever claim to be

completely unbiased or detached we must assume that some colouring is always present. It is the degree of its influence which is important. Remember that all these questions apply particularly if *you* are the channel. Honest answers will show you the areas you need to work on within yourself.

Colouring of this kind means that you should be aware of the need to make allowances. Never follow guidance blindly and always stop to think whether any advice on which you plan to act is in tune with your own intuition and integrity.

It is surprising how many seemingly sane, balanced and wise people will suddenly do things entirely out of character or for glaringly wrong reasons just because a discarnate entity, with doubtful credentials, channelled through a fallible human being, has said so.

From time to time wise guides, channelled at a very high level, may urge you to take calculated risks. If these are in line with your creative vision and are the prompt or permission you needed, then your life may change for the better as a result. If such suggestions are ungrounded in reality or are made without due regard for current responsibilities, then acting on them may mean that some hard lessons are learned.

The higher guides are rarely stern, dogmatic, domineering, peremptory or over-directive. A message someone once reported receiving from a guide was: 'You've got everything wrong. You have made a mess of your life. Pack your bags *today* and go to Australia. You *must* obey, otherwise there will be no more help.'

Even making allowances for colouring this is not the voice of a true, higher guide. Imagine that you are really in a desperate situation; you have come for guidance as a last resort; you are feeling a failure, blaming yourself and are full of guilt. You have no connections in Australia and have rarely travelled anywhere. Now, if you do not obey this peremptory directive you are threatened with being cut off from all possible spiritual help. The effects of such a message could be dangerous and devastating. Part of the responsibility of the co-operative and more conscious channelling of the Aquarian Age is for the channel to make sure that such messages do not get through.

How different the picture is if the enquirer is told: 'You have been through a very difficult period of heavy learning but now is a good time to gather your resources and make a fresh start. Consider all your options – perhaps even a completely new venture or horizon. Value what you have learned from the past. Try to see that what you are now calling mistakes are also learning opportunities for yourself and others. You will not need to learn these lessons again. Do not let the past and your regrets about it hold you back. Look to the future and step into it with confidence, but at your own pace. We are always here to help and your guardian angel never ceases to watch over you.'

Although, when analysed, the message has some similar elements, it is expressed in a loving, supportive and compassionate way. The enquirer is given freedom, hope, encouragement and assured of non-judgemental acceptance. These are always the key notes of the true guides. You may long to be told exactly what to do, but guides are not there to live your life for you. They offer themselves as companions and friends who see a wider perspective from which they can offer a new vision and wise counsel. The responsibility for choice and action must always remain your own.

A more positive aspect of colouring is that which gives a particular guide special characteristics. All the higher guides have a great sense of humour. Many will adopt certain phrases, and tones, or subtly manifest traits and style which make them very identifiable. Gildas is gentle. He is often a master of understatement. When he knows a group or individual to have lost any first awe of him, he will gently tease or make humorous comments on things happening in the outer environment.

Other guides are energetic, inspire their channels to wide gestures, or challenge their audiences in order to provoke discussion or thought. All these things can be accomplished without the guidance being dogmatic or negatively critical.

Vocabulary

In conscious co-operative channelling or mediumship the guide can only use the vocabulary of the channel. Words which are rarely used ordinarily by the channel will emerge from hidden places, there will be different turns of phrase, the guide will coin characteristic expressions – but the words used are all within the medium's knowledge.

An example from my own experience happened when a group of healers using specialist techniques and terminology asked me to channel some advice from Gildas. While more general questions were being asked all went well, but when we moved into the specialist field insufficient information seemed to be available. Gildas then explained that the problem was one of vocabularly. I spent a day learning some specific terms and then the full answers required were forthcoming.

Authority issues and conditioning

Throughout our lives we feel constrained to please others. Parents, teachers, society, eventually even parts of our inner selves, all demand some form of obedience or conformity. Compliance is the norm. We expect to be given examples and precepts on which to model ourselves.

Few of us are totally pleased with our lives. When we become parents, we try to prevent our children from making the mistakes we have made. We push our children to achieve where we failed and to become that which we longed to be. We look at society and try to groom our offspring to fit the roles which society demands or rewards the most. We forget that we probably learned little from our parents' mistakes. Children, from a very early age, are distinct universes with their own blueprints. We give the best upbringing when we are continually alert to find what the blueprint may be, and to encourage and nurture it.

The dissatisfactions we have with our own lives are largely due to seeking approval, living out others' expectations and succumbing to conditioning which is not fully in tune with our true selves. Before we know where we are, we are guilty of perpetuating the system. With horror we hear, coming out of our own mouths, to our own children, the very statements which made us squirm when our own parents said them to us:

'I had to conform to my parents'/teachers' wishes and it never did me any harm.'

'I went to a strictly disciplinarian school and learned to toe the line – it wasn't such a bad thing.'

If we really consider such statements we may realise the hurt which underlies them. Sometimes fear of facing that pain is the cause of our sustaining the very structures we inwardly despise.

Some conformity is necessary to the smooth running of society, but blind, unquestioning obedience is dangerous. It encourages politics of power rather than ensuring caring government and nurturing of individual talents. If we conform or obey without question we hand over self-responsibility and deny ourselves choices. We sit back and blame the authorities – the all powerful 'they' – without recourse to our rights to have a say in who 'they' are and how 'they' should act. The macrocosm reflects the microcosm and vice versa.

Sub-personalities

When entering any growth process involving self-knowledge you soon become aware of the complexity of your inner psychological mechanisms. What lies behind the use of the pronoun 'I'?

'I am a woman/man.'

'I like swimming.'

'I am a teacher.'

'I am married/single' ... and so on.

You may also say:

'Part of me wants to go swimming and part doesn't.'

'Part of me likes tidiness, but another part is just a slut.'

'Sometimes when I want to have fun, part of me holds back.'

'I am very hard on myself.'

'My spiteful, jealous side sometimes betrays me.'

'How could I have behaved like that and said those rude things at that time?'

Usually when you say 'I', the part you know, trust and with which you identify is speaking. When you explore yourself further you may find, either to your delight or consternation, that you are legion.

The Italian psychologist Assagioli formulated the system of self-analysis known as psychosynthesis (see Bibliography). He named the different aspects of ourselves 'sub-personalities'. Earlier, Jung had spoken of the persona or mask. Our working and professional selves or personas are usually very different from our relaxed, private or holiday selves. We, and those with whom we live and work, need these masks, which help us to play the many different roles life demands of us. We even wear certain uniforms to help the persona to operate. The pin-striped suit for business, the apron for housework, the sporting gear for jogging, the T-shirt for relaxation, the formal or beautiful clothes for entertaining and party-going are all supports for essential aspects of our day-to-day interactions.

In some ways the concept of the sub-personality goes further than that of the persona and refers to the deeper dynamics at work within the psyche. We use the persona more consciously. The sub-personalities develop as a result of conditioning and can be survival mechanisms. They are distinctive energies within the psyche. Ferrucci, a disciple of Assagioli, refers to them as 'degraded archetypes' (see Bibliography).

Angels represent the pure energy of the archetypes of higher qualities. In order to relate to the pure archetypal emanations you first need to name the energies (see page 19).

Naming, however, is not enough. You also need symbols in your search for right relationship with these great forces. Most of the archetypes of higher qualities have universally recognised symbols: the dove and olive branch for Peace; the scales for Justice; the scales weighing the feather of truth for Truth; Aphrodite emerging from the sea on a shell for Beauty; the Caduceus (two snakes twined round a staff) for Healing; the heart for Love; the throne and sceptre for Power and so on.

Yet even these powerful symbols are not enough to aid your grasp of the forces which move you. You need a further breakdown into component parts which leads to personification. The Tarot is an ancient system of divination which uses 22 archetypal personifications (see Glossary).

Such images also help an awareness of the shadow or degraded aspect of the archetypes. Peace is shadowed by war or unrest; Justice by injustice; Truth by deceit; Beauty by ugliness; Healing or Health by disease; Love by hate; and Power by tyranny.

Conditioning influences often derive from degraded or misinterpreted archetypal forces. In order to deal with the growth difficulties inflicted in this way we ingest or inwardly create the degraded archetypes which are our sub-personalities. They usually manifest as pairs of opposites.

People who have been required to be over-orderly in childhood will probably have an obsessively tidy sub-personality but also one which is disordered and chaotic; people who have been subject to power and manipulation may have an inner tyrant but also an inner victim; people who have been required to be too 'good', may have an inner 'goody goody' or strict moralist, but also a naughty, devious, dishonest or sly sub-personality.

These pairs perpetuate each other and until you work with them, they will remain largely in your unconscious mind where they become autonomous and somewhat disso-ciated. They may emerge to surprise and embarrass you in unexpected situations, particularly when you are under stress. Your friends may remark, 'I've not really seen that side of you before. Your behaviour at that party/meeting/ encounter was quite a revelation.'

Fortunately sub-personalities are rewarding to work with. They reveal themselves readily when you seek them out. When they tell their stories and help you to understand what they seek and why they have developed, they become important allies in the journey to self-knowledge. The exer-cise at the end of this chapter will help you.

Knowing your sub-personalities gives you insight into the vulnerable areas of your make-up which may give rise to colouring in the guidance which channels or influences your interpretation of guidance you have sought.

Sub-personalities, before being recognised and so begin-ning their journey to integration, may make it difficult to see clearly another aspect of yourself; an aspect often referred to as 'the inner wise being' or presence.

There are moments in life when you feel that you are

complete. The different parts are not pulling you in different directions. You are able to speak or act from a point of
inner wisdom or integrity. You know that you are 'on
truth'. The search for self-growth is a search for integration,
the state in which you know all your parts, your weaknesses
and your strengths. Then, when you stand firm at the centre
and say 'I', you can feel, without inflation, the richness and
power which is behind that simple pronoun.

Part of your search for angelic or discarnate guidance is
also a search for the true self. It is difficult to be told that
you get the clearest discarnate or outer guidance only when
you are able to connect with the inner wise presence. Many
people say 'But if that were so, I would not need a guide'.
There are many challenging spiritual paradoxes. This is one
of them. First find the inner wisdom; conscious contact with
higher discarnate guides and other planes will follow.

Higher guides seek to protect as well as to communicate
with you. They know that you will be at your least vulnerable and least subject to confusing colouring when you
commune with them not only from a place of inner peace
but of inner wisdom. This is why the meeting place meditation on page 38 and the inner wise presence meditation
on page 57 are of vital and basic importance.

When you meet guides or angels at a high level you are
automatically protected from unwanted interference. When
your inner wise self meets with your higher guides then a
truly creative contact is made. From this a different perspective on life's meaning and its dilemmas can emerge.

Expectations and mind set

The expectations you have of your guides, how you imagine
they will appear or the manner in which you await their
communications can be obstacles to the process of guidance.

If you expect something to manifest in a certain form you
can undervalue or blind yourself to what else may be

appearing. It is tempting to compare and evaluate. I have worked with people receiving high quality guidance but refusing to take it seriously because it is not according to a preconceived model.

'It is not like Gildas,' they will say.

'A. seems to have a much clearer way of communicating with his guide.'

'I feel my guide's presence – it is beautiful – but I don't *see* anyone.'

'All I get is symbols. I never hear a voice.'

'Whenever I ask for help it always comes, I meet the right person at the right time, read the right book or get an unexpected letter – but is this really guidance?'

Models

It is important to beware of being attached to, or influenced by, particular models of guidance you admire, to the degree that you fail to recognise or value your own individual and unique model.

The guidance I get from Gildas and being there to receive it is a life's work. The model it gives can be confusing. It can also be a cause of subconscious resistance if others see or take the picture of my relationship with Gildas as being representative of what all channelling necessarily requires. It can provoke anxious questions:

'Will my guide demand a life's dedication?'

'Will I be able to deal with the changes in my life which discovering my guide might demand of me?

The misgivings underlying such questions can cause subtle

blockages to the surrender which is required for the phenomenon of channelling.

Surrender in the moment, however, does not mean life surrender. No one is required to give more to guides and guidance than they are prepared to give. Guides are not authority figures who must be obeyed unquestioningly. As they get to know you they will offer you choices. *Real* choices. Control of the degree of your involvement is always in *your* hands.

Constantly review your motives for seeking fuller contact with your guides. They offer you new dimensions to life and sometimes make you aware of previously unrecognised choices. Gildas often reminds me, 'Be careful what you ask for. The likelihood is that you will get it'.

Once expectations are released you can begin to be the co-designer of your own model of guidance. You can ask your guide to help with your spiritual training and awareness, but you can also take a part in training your guide.

This last point is important. Guides are beyond the human time dimension. They do not want to intrude on your time or make your life inconvenient. They do not expect you to give them pride of place and neglect other activities or responsibilities. It always concerns me when I see someone running hither and thither at their guide's beck and call. People with inner authority issues may be particularly vulnerable. Conversations are stopped, meals abandoned and sleep disturbed as the general structure of life falls apart.

'My guide tweaks my ear and then I *have* to take time alone to listen.'

'My guide wakes me at 3 a.m. and I have to write down what is being said.'

'I'm never allowed to go to bed before 1 a.m. My guide will only communicate then, when the house is quiet.'

Such attitudes are dangerous and out of proportion. To

ensure that life continues normally, though enhanced by guidance, dialogue with the guide is necessary. State your availability with confidence.

'I am able to devote time to this work for an hour every morning/evening/week/fortnight/month. I will keep that appointment as carefully as I would any other. If you want to speak to me at other times, let us agree a sign. I cannot interrupt normal living but I will make time to tune in as soon as possible after receiving such a sign.'

Eventually you or your guide may want to increase the frequency or length of the times you give to developing the contact. Any agreement must be mutual and you should never feel pressurised or coerced.

The establishment of signals should be an early part of the training. While you may put boundaries on the times when you should be called, your guide will rarely pose similar restrictions upon you. In times of necessity it is important to have a means of showing your guide that you need to make contact.

The meeting place meditation (see page 38) is part of this process. The meditation on page 60 takes this some stages further, and includes important work with signs and signals.

Any guide who continues to invade the general structure of life without due cause should be under suspicion. If this happens to you it may be necessary to seek advice. But, first of all, honestly review your authority issues. Ask yourself whether you associate guidance with a certain amount of drama or glamour, whether you are making yourself 'special' or becoming precious in your spiritual seeking.

Ways in which guidance manifests

When you take time to review your life (see pages 7–8), the hand of guidance – or is it destiny? – can be clearly seen.

At crucial life points you make one choice rather than another. A set of circumstances ensures that you arrive in a certain place at a certain time. Even accidents and illnesses play a part in shaping the pattern. You may look back with disappointment, resentment, frustration or resignation. You may wish that the fates had dealt you a better hand. Usually a definitive pattern can be perceived. Part of the growth process is recognising that you can take a more conscious part in your own destiny. Indeed you have to play the hand you have been dealt. Studying the cards and playing them skilfully makes a big difference to the quality and meaning of life.

Destiny does not mean that every aspect of your life is preordained. The aim of life is to gain experience. Your higher self knows what range of learning will be of most value to your soul. By choice of historical time, culture, parents, abilities and the body in which you incarnate, your individual range is limited. Within those limitations, unless you deliberately and forcefully insist on following an evil path, there are no wrong choices. In the highest sense, whatever is happening to you, you are in the right place at the right time. As soon as you recognise this you will be able to see more clearly the wider guidance of your higher self. Specific guidance from guides, angels or your inner wise being will then foster and enable the most positive use of your opportunities. You will also be assisted, where necessary, to change your attitudes so that a more creative approach to life can blossom.

Working to have conscious communication with guides and angels means that you can be encouraged by a pertinent commentary on the things which puzzle or confuse you. You can always have access to comfort and wise counsel, and be given a wider perspective to prevent you from being hemmed or blocked in.

When you make it clear that you are open and ready for guidance it will come through symbols, words, synchronicities or the right connection at the right time. Subtle permissions, coupled with non-judgemental support, will strengthen your confidence and self-image so that you feel you are working consistently towards reaching and accepting your full potential.

In order for the signs of guidance to become clearer you must be neither over-active nor over-passive. Too much sense of urgency will make you blind to the true messages your guides are trying to communicate. Too much passivity will mean that you miss opportunities. Waiting to be pushed can be a means of evading your responsibility for choice. Gildas has said:

'Sometimes it is necessary for guidance to come from knocks on the head and kicks from behind. This is not as we really wish it to be.'

It is too true that sometimes a major or minor 'disaster' is necessary to shift people out of set positions. Asking for, and learning to perceive, guidance enables life to become less of an obstacle course.

If you have asked for guidance, expect it to come but be open to the ways in which it may do so for, besides direct written or spoken communication, they are many: coming across the right book at the right time; reading an article in the dentist's waiting room; overhearing a conversation on the bus; a cancelled meeting which opens up another opportunity are just a few examples.

It is important not to get into the condition where you see meaning in every nuance or develop a kind of 'superstition'. Nevertheless, belief that your guides and guardians can speak to you through daily events, coincidences and synchronicities gives you a creativity, receptivity and alertness which is essential to wise and guided living.

Exercise 8
Working with the Inner Wise Being and Sub-Personalities

The unconscious or semi-conscious presence of troublesome sub-personalities may block clear access to your inner wise being.

As you work with the sub-personalities the connections to wisdom will improve. Yet since the inner wise being is always somewhere within your make-up, you should do the exercise for connecting with its presence before the sub-personality exercise. The inner wise being can then witness your exploration of your sub-personalities, both protecting you and growing stronger in itself throughout the process.

Sub-personalities can appear in a multitude of forms – as stereo-typed people, as animals, birds, mythical creatures or cartoon characters. Usually they communicate willingly, clearly telling their stories and what they may require of you. They will also, with your help, communicate with each other. Eventually they may outlive their purpose and fade away, they may change into valued inner allies or they may merge and blend with each other, making your inner family or personnel less numerous and unwiedly.

(a) Guided journey to contact your inner wise being or presence

Make sure that you will be undisturbed and provide yourself with a rug or blanket for warmth, then find a relaxed but balanced and supported position for your body … Close your eyes … Be aware of the rhythm of your breathing and bring that rhythm into your heart centre, thus activating the heart energy on which to travel into your inner landscape … Find yourself in a meadow … Activate all your inner senses so that you see the objects and colours, hear the sounds, touch the textures, smell the fragrances and savour the tastes …

Be aware of your inner landscape around and beyond the meadow … Know that somewhere in this landscape your inner wise presence dwells … You can either journey to that dwelling-place for a part of you knows well how to find the pathway … Or you can call the wise presence towards you now, in the meadow …

At your journey's goal or when you call you may experience an atmosphere of wise understanding, see colours, hear a beau-tiful sound, smell a special fragrance or meet with a being … As you either experience this presence or see your inner wise being, ask for a blessing on your inner life and your search for contact with guides and angels ...

You may receive a special gift or talisman for use in this work, be given a key-word, feel a lightening of your heart or a knowledge that you are guided and protected ... If you receive none of these, then know that there will be other opportunities to meet with your wise presence, and that this initial journey has been important in paving the way ...

Spend up to ten minutes enjoying the company of your inner wise presence and then, if you have journeyed beyond it, return to your meadow ... To the rhythm of your breathing in your heart centre ... To your awareness of your body, your contact with the ground and your normal surroundings ... Imagine that there is a cloak of light with a hood right around you ... Take your pencils, pens and crayons, and record your journey.

(b) Guided journey to contact some sub-personalities

Make the same preparations for your comfort and protection from disturbance as you did in Exercise 8(a).

Note that this journey provides a chance for you to meet not more than four sub-personalities who may have any bearing on your work with guides and angels. On subsequent occasions you can ask to meet four more sub-personalities, but it is wise to limit the number to four at any one time. The only exception to this rule would be the discovery that you have a sub-personality manifesting as twins or in some other way having an inseparable counterpart. Such pairs count as one sub-personality. (One client had a bat and ball, for instance.)

Close your eyes ... Be aware of the rhythm of your breathing and bring that rhythm into your heart centre, thus activating the heart energy on which to travel into your inner landscape ... Find yourself in the meadow ... And activate all your inner senses so that you see the objects and colours, hear the sounds, touch the textures, smell the fragrances and taste the tastes.

Call your inner wise presence into the meadow and ask for its company on your journey to the place where your sub-personalities dwell ...Take with you any special object or talisman which helps you to 'centre' and to feel protected ... (see Glossary).

Somewhere in your inner landscape, maybe quite close to the meadow, there is a river ... Carrying or wearing your talisman and accompanied by your inner wise presence, journey now to the river ...

As you walk beside the river you will become aware that nearby there is a quiet backwater or tributary stream ...Anchored on this backwater or stream is a houseboat – the home of your sub-personalities ...

As you draw nearer to the boat you may be aware of the activity and noise of your sub-personalities ...

Stand back and observe the boat ...What sort of a boat is it? ...What is its state of repair and upkeep? ...What are the arrangements for boarding and landing? ...

After this initial inspection withdraw a little from the bank and find a comfortable place in which to sit while keeping the boat in full view ... Choose a sunwarmed spot and rest your back against a tree or rock ... Be aware of your inner wise presence supporting you ...

Ask that not more than four sub-personalities from the houseboat prepare to reveal themselves to you ... On this occasion they should be any aspects of yourself who might in any way be blocking your ability to work with guides and angels, or who might be responsible for colouring the quality of any communications you are likely to receive ...

Insist that the sub-personalities reveal themselves to you one at a time ... When you have met and greeted the first it should step to one side as you greet the next ...The second should then step back as you greet the third and the third should make way, in its turn, for the fourth ...

Observe and greet each sub-personality, and let them also observe and greet you ... Ask each one to tell you their story in brief (how and when they came into being, what they fear, what they require at this time) ...

When you have met these sub-personalities, reflect whether

you sense that any two of them need to talk to each other ... Also ask your inner wise presence to give advice ... Do not put the dialogue into effect on this occasion, merely become aware of what might be of value ...

Before asking your sub-personalities to return to the house-boat consider whether you are willing to make any commitment to further work with them ...

(You could consider returning to this place for further dialogue; any requests from your sub-personalities as to their present needs; returning to this place to enable any two sub-personalities to dialogue together; agreeing that you will give something which it requires to a sub-personality, in exchange for something you require from it. Use your creativity and growing understanding of these mechanisms to find ways of modifying their weaknesses and autonomy or of harnessing their strengths. Do not commit your-self to anything you will be unable to carry out in the near future.)

Finally, thank your sub-personalities for revealing themselves and ask them to return to the houseboat, giving them any reassurances or promises of further work which you feel able to give ...

When the sub-personalities are safely aboard, journey back to the meadow, accompanied by your inner wise presence ...

From the meadow return to the rhythm of your breathing in your heart centre ... To your awareness of your body, your contact with the ground and your normal surroundings ... Imagine that there is a cloak of light with a hood right around you ... Take your pencils, pens and crayons, and record your journey.

Exercise 9
Revisiting the Meeting Place with a Power Animal and Your Inner Wise Presence. Establishing Signs and Signals

Power animals

Animals are significant allies in your inner world. They can help and guard you when you are doing work which entails possible altered states of consciousness and exploration of other realities. In the inner worlds creatures who, in the present conditions of the everyday material world would be wild, fierce or unapproachable, are friends. They readily communicate, come when you call, and offer healing, comfort and protection. Calling an animal to you means that all your instinctual qualities and perceptions are alert. In the Native American tradition they are called power or medicine animals. As you work in the inner worlds you will probably find that there are a number of animals who come to you for different purposes, such as healing, guardianship, comfort, aiding communication and loving companionship.

In this core meditation for the development of guidance you are given an opportunity to meet with the power animal who will be 'the guardian of your threshold', making your journeys to other realms and planes extra safe, and as smooth as possible.

Signs and signals

In the spiritual realms there is a sacred law of three: ask for something three times and it will usually be granted. One of the ways in which guidance manifests is for something, such as a book you should read, to be brought to your attention three times in a short period. When working with a guide it is important to establish a recognition sign or signal which is the seal of genuineness. When your guide approaches that sign will be shown, withdrawn, shown again, withdrawn and shown for a third time. No false or lower guide can abuse the sacred law of three and so cannot maintain a threefold signal in this way. The sign may be a gesture, a fragrance, a colour, a symbol or a key-word. When you reach the level of consciousness represented by the plateau, there is comparatively little need to challenge your guides for genuineness and integrity as it is difficult for false or lower guides to function here but it is important to build in the call sign as a tool or discipline. It is not always possible to check your level of consciousness and there may be occasions when your guide will come closer to the material realms to contact you at a point where interference or psychic 'noise' might be around.

The journey

Making sure that you will be undisturbed, sit or lie in a comfortable, but symmetrically balanced, position. Have ready a blanket for warmth, and crayons and paper for any recording you may wish to do.

Be aware of the rhythm of your breathing ... Gradually bring that rhythm into your heart centre or chakra ...

Travel on the heart energy into your inner landscape and find yourself, once more, in the meadow ... Activate all your inner senses so that you see the objects and colours, smell the fragrances, hear the sounds, touch the textures and savour the tastes ...

Invoke the presence of your inner wise being and have with you any special object or talisman you wish to take on this journey ... Look out at the surrounding landscape and see a wooded area, perhaps in a slight valley, having about it a special quality of deep green lushness ... It is here that your power animal guardian of the threshold dwells ... Within the forest there may be a rocky area with some caves or some of the great trees may have holes at the base of their trunks as accommodation for your animal ...

Accompanied by your inner wise being, journey to the forest area and call your animal to come to you ... Remember that this creature is your friend and ally, even though it may be one of the big cats, a wolf or a normally deadly snake ... Greet your animal and ask it to accompany you on the next part of the journey.

Emerge from the forest to a place where you can see the winding pathway which leads into the hills and continues up into the mountains ...

Take this pathway, knowing that you are going to the plateau which is near the top of one of the mountains, but not beyond the tree line ...

At the plateau, refresh yourself from the source of clear running water ... Find again your sanctuary or meeting place, and settle yourself comfortably with your inner wise presence and your animal guardian nearby ... Breathe into your heart chakra so that your heart energy continues to flow strongly ... Have a sense of open expectation ...

In your heart speak an invitation or invocation for your guide to appear ... Assert your readiness for this contact ...

Be aware that a being may appear in a particular dress, from a particular geographic area or historical time (see page 13) ...

Be equally aware that your guide may come in a body of light and colour, as a fragrance or merely as a sense of another energy being present with you ... In whatever form your guide elects to appear you should feel a sense of openness and peace ... There may be some excitement and a little anxiety, but the very ambience of your guide's presence should be reassuring and comforting ...

Ask now for a signal or sign to be shown and clearly repeated three times ...

When the signal has been given greet your guide and ask any questions you may have in your mind ... At this point you might like to ask for a name for your guide ... Remember that you may get a response in words, symbols or inner knowing ... You may only get a sense of continuing peace ... In this case trust that in the next few days there will be synchronicities or coincidences in your life which will evoke the answers or guidance you seek ...

Stay here for not more than 15 minutes ... When you are ready to return, drink again from the water source at this plateau ... Accompanied by your power animal and your inner wise presence make your way back to the meadow ...

Take leave of your companions in the meadow ... Return to the awareness of your breath in your heart centre ... To the consciousness of your body and your contact with the ground ... To your outer surroundings ... Visualise a cloak of light with a hood, right around you ...

Take time to record your journey in words or drawing ...

Return to your everyday routines.

6

LIVING WITH ANGELS

Angels as ever-present allies ... Activities which help to bring angels closer and promote their work ... Crystals, sound, fragrance and angels ... From gravity to levity ... Car parking angels ... The angels of transmutation ... The simplest, most comprehensive invocation ... How angels communicate ... Exercises 10 and 11.

Angels as ever-present allies

We are not used to acknowledging the presence of angels in our lives, yet they are always with us. It is not only when we are making major life decisions, taking risks or in peril, that our guardian angel is near. He hovers constantly around us as we perform all the mundane tasks of daily living.

When we sleep, Michael and his helpers, guardians of the night and bringers of dreams, watch over us. They endeavour to ensure that our bodies and minds receive beneficial rest and sleep. They cleanse the air we breathe and renew our spirits.

When the sun rises and morning breaks, Uriel and his supporters help us to awaken. They nurture the fire energy within us so that we can be ready to use the day creatively, whatever it may bring.

At noon, Gabriel and his retinue replenish our hope.

They activate the water element within us so that we can flow with life, digest our food and be in touch with our feelings without being overwhelmed by emotion.

As evening approaches Raphael and his angelic helpers bless our recreational activities and relaxation. They enhance our connection to the good things of earth and aid us in finding joy in incarnation. They will help us as we review the day we have lived, bring us comfort for life's trials and healing for our bodies.

Acknowledging the flow of help and life-force from the angels will help you to keep things in perspective and to be more positive. All you need do is give them a mental greeting or silently express your gratitude. Formal invocations (see page 26) help the angels to forge a stronger connection with you. As you feel the power of your ability to invoke, you open up to the angelic qualities and may have vivid experiences of their light and presence. But this method only needs to be used from time to time. For daily use, a mental acknowledgement, an inward prayer or silently worded request are sufficient.

- An appeal to Michael at bedtime will activate his care and guardianship, and ease you into sleep.
- Asking for Uriel's blessing will make mornings less of a bugbear.
- Requesting Gabriel's grace at noon will encourage you to maintain a positive attitude to life and maintain your stamina.
- In the evening, a thought to Raphael will ease your tensions, bringing a sense of healing and peace.

Angels are connected with earth, air, fire and water. Whenever you use the elements, angels will be present taking an active part. Remember this can make even the washing up become an exciting and light-filled activity.

Rather than setting aside 20 minutes or an hour each day for meditational observance, most exponents of meditation agree that the ideal is to bring a meditative quality to the whole of life. Angels help you to do this as you find spirit in matter and joy in the mundane.

Shower with the angels

Next time you take a bath or shower, be aware of the angelic light in the water. You will emerge very much more refreshed.

Taking care of your body and performing even the most basic bodily functions means that the earth angels are present. Acknowledging this can bring a greater conscious appreciation of the daily miracles which your body accomplishes.

Shop and eat with the angels

When you eat or drink, particularly of that which is natural and wholesome, angels are present to aid your digestion. Awareness of this makes it much easier to avoid junk foods and unhealthy eating patterns. When you shop, take the angels with you and see what a difference they make to the contents of your supermarket trolley.

In these days of casual eating and rejection of religious dogma, few meals are prayerfully blessed. The blessing of food is not only a religious observance. It activates angelic light and power which energises and purifies what you are about to eat. People who can see the aura or energy field of food, report that before blessing, modern food, polluted with chemicals and often forced into growth out of season, can be very lacking in life-force. After blessing, a miracle occurs. The energy field of the food becomes pure, faster in vibration and full of light. Such fare is not only more nourishing, but means that you ingest less toxins and environmental pollution. Ask a silent, mental, blessing on each meal, or briefly pass your hands over the food you have prepared, inviting the angels to bless and cleanse it.

Breathe with the angels

Today we worry, with good reason, about the quality of the air we breathe. Again the angels can help. It must be remembered that angels function best in the material world when, by acknowledging them, we build a bridge of consciousness which enables them to be more tangibly present. When you inhale and exhale with an awareness of the angels of air, you ingest fewer toxins and draw a purer life-force into your lungs. Even five minutes a day of conscious breathing with the angels makes a difference.

Angels of fire

All angels are beautiful but the brightly active angels of the fire element are particularly attractive. They are distressed by the prevalent, widespread, addiction to smoking, but love hearth fires and the use of candles. Lighting a candle each morning for attunement and focus sets the day into spiritual perspective, and helps to activate the network of light consciousness on earth. The fire angels particularly love such a ritual. If you decide to incorporate this into your daily practices or for occasional ceremonies and celebrations remember to give a special acknowledgement to the angels of the fire element.

The fire element is particularly active in the digestion and metabolism of food. If you have digestive or metabolic problems a thought to the angels of fire could bring relief.

Conception and contraception

The act of sexual love draws a variety of angelic light into action. The moment a child is conceived is especially blessed by the angels of fire. When you wish to conceive a child, a formal invocation to the angels of fire will enhance fertility and help you to find the right moment for conception. On the other hand, if you are practising contraception the angels of the water element will aid its efficiency.

In almost every daily pursuit angels, the devas and the elementals who work with them will be at hand. The more you remember to acknowledge or ask for their involvement the more vivid will their presence in your life become. Some activities positively promote the presence of angels, ensuring that they bring their healing, inspiration and light more palpably into your reality.

Activities which help to bring angels closer and promote their work

Tending the garden and growing house plants draws the earth angels closer.

Loving and caring contact with animals and young children is blessed by the angels of tenderness.

Creating cleanliness and harmony in your home or work environment evokes the angels of harmony. Using colour well, placing a beautiful, but not necessarily expensive, object as a focal point, having flowers and plants, even in the office or workplace, are small but effective ways of bringing angelic light closer.

The angels of beauty, inspiration, creativity and reverence are present when you appreciate music, literature, art, architecture and the loveliness of nature. The harmonies and creation of music are inspired by angels. This is true not only of the great classics, but also of much popular music. Unfortunately some music, which has some very negative rhythm patterns, has made an appearance during recent years. This music particularly unsettles young people even though they are often drawn to it. Too much of it – especially at too high a volume – generates or exacerbates tendencies to violence. When such music is heard the angels of transmutation need to be called in. (For more on this see page 74.)

Being creative, from cooking through artistic activities to creative decision making, activates the angels of creativity. Stimulating conversation and the exchange of ideas attracts the angels of mental creativity and wisdom. They foster the ability to govern ourselves and the world with wisdom, and bring inspiration and balance to our thinking.

Having fun attracts the angels of humour, fun, delight and celebration. We make far too little use of the art of celebration. There is no need to wait for the special occasion and lavish setting. If you can find something to celebrate, even in difficult times, angels will be your allies as you guard yourself against depression and nurture your ability to find meaning in life.

Many adults lose the capacity for play in the truly creative sense. We play games or get involved in sports. If there are children around we may become involved in more spontaneously playful activities, but few adults will buy themselves a balloon, a kite, a packet of stick-on stars and shapes or a pot of soapy bubble-making liquid just for the delight of it. Do not look down on such activities with a jaundiced eye, but relax, forget care for a while and enjoy the angels of play.

Problems often take on a different perspective after half an hour's sheer playfulness. Play and creativity go together. A mini holiday from serious thought clears the way for the elusive solution or new idea to surface. But play has a real importance in its own right. It is another means of strengthening the bridge between angels and humans.

All angels bring with them a sense of love, but if one species of angels can be said to be more important than another then it is the angels of love. When we have open hearts the force of love flows and connects us to the angels of love so that their much needed qualities become more active in our world.

Sexual activity is often described as 'making love'. What a happily apt term this is! When human beings celebrate sexual intimacy, the angels of love, closely accompanied by the angels of sensuality, laughter, tenderness, warmth, passion, creativity and celebration crowd in, generating rainbows of light energy.

Colour, crystals, sound, fragrance and angels

Angels create the wonder of colour. Their light bodies vibrate with vivid, translucent rainbow hues as they carry waves of colour towards us. When you use colour harmoniously angels crowd in. They especially love translucent colours.

The ancient builders of cathedrals such as Chartres, in France, knew the power of translucent colour. The stained glass windows of Chartres cathedral have a special quality which attracts angelic presences.

Arranging beautifully coloured and shaped glass bottles where light can shine through them ensures a more active angelic presence in your home. Colour has great healing power. The angels of healing can work with especial effectiveness when you use colours of such translucency.

Cut glass crystals, hung in a sunny window, produce abundant rainbows of light. As sunlight filters through them the room becomes filled with angels and dancing elementals.

Real crystals, such as clear quartz, amethyst, rose quartz and aventurine, are reminders to us of the spirit which resides in matter. A few crystals in your living space will attract angels. You can dedicate a crystal to help your awareness of angels in general or your guardian angel in particular (see page 78). If you are uncertain which crystals to choose, a good crystal book should be consulted (see Bibliography). Clear quartz crystals have the whole spectrum of colour within them and make excellent personal crystals. Amethysts bring close the angels of protection. Rose quartz opens the heart centre, and attracts the angels of love and tenderness.

Green crystals will help you to contact the Archangel Gabriel. Use these if you need hope, healing for a dysfunctional family, special protection for women and children or if you want to increase your appreciation of the element of water.

Yellow crystals will activate contact with the Archangel

Uriel. They will clarify your mind, and aid your relationship with the worlds of science, politics and social reform. They are especially helpful when you want to find a clear direction in life. The more orangey yellow or sunshine coloured crystals connect you to the element of fire and enhance your creativity.

Red crystals will aid connection with the Archangel Raphael. Use them to nurture your spiritual, psychological and physical growth, when you are undergoing emotional stress or in need of any kind of healing. They will increase your connection with the element of earth. In the world of crystals, black crystals are part of the red family and can be used for the same purposes.

Blue crystals will draw the Archangel Michael towards you. Use them to aid your dreams, soothe night-time fears and bring about transformation in your life. Blue crystals will enhance your connection with the element of air, help you to communicate well and bring you inner peace.

The angelic connection with music has already been mentioned (see page 68), but there are some special sounds which attract the angels. These are Tibetan bells and singing bowls, rain sticks, drums and the human voice. Particular mantra or chants such as '*Aum mani padme aum*', sung by a single voice or group of voices, can bring a whole flood of angelic presences to a room or group.

Burning joss sticks or essential oils in the environment or inhaling the beautiful natural fragrances of flowers and trees will also aid your closeness to angels.

From gravity to levity

Gravity is the physical phenomenon or force-field which keeps us on the earth without spinning off to hurtle into outer space. At the same time the word gravity means seriousness, weight and importance.

Perhaps because humans are so dependent on the law of gravity we have become serious, heavy and self-important.

Dogmatic religions have portrayed the spiritual path as grave, serious and weighty, but contact with angels brings lightness, zest, adventure and pleasure to the spiritual journey.

The task of some of the angels of qualities might be seen as grave, serious or weighty. There are angels of responsibility, education, efficiency, willingness, order, work, discipline, forgiveness, honesty, compassion, truth, dedication, commitment, justice, concentration and constraint. They do not carry a goad with which to prick our consciences but, instead, bring us these qualities as blessings. If you want to be efficient or disciplined you must beseech the angels of efficiency and discipline to give you their grace.

Angels are not bound by gravity. They are beings of levity or lightness. Some bring the serious qualities by which they are named. It is we, not the angels, who take life so seriously. The angels who carry the heavier qualities do so for us. If we allow them to do so, they will teach us to give all aspects of life a lighter touch so that we can also enjoy the angels of light, delight, fun, humour, joy, pleasure, freedom, release, abundance, spontaneity, celebration, excitement, wonder, love, pleasure, laughter, openness, opportunity, adventure and synchronicity.

I have angelic qualities written out on cards (see Exercise 10, below). When I am feeling inefficient or undisciplined, I draw the cards for these angels and put them on my desk. I try to remember that they are not there to strengthen my will-power but to make my approach to these attributes easier and lighter. If I reach the right attitude – 'I invoke and celebrate the presence of the angel of efficiency today' – minor miracles occur. If I look at those cards and think 'These are reminders to me to be efficient because I am such a slut,' I drop more piles of paper, spill more cups of coffee and generally create more inefficiency than usual. If I trust the angel's presence, I move from the grave burden of efficiency to a consciousness of levity and ease. An invisible oil is poured over troubled waters. Efficiency, so lightly attained, leaves more time and inclination for play.

Car parking angels

The angels of synchronicity who are active in many areas of life deserve a special mention. The *Chambers* dictionary definition of synchronicity is: 'To coincide or agree in time; *to cause to coincide or agree in time*; to time together or to a standard' (my italics).

I have emphasised the second part of the definition as being closest to the function which angels of synchronicity and our guides often use in order to bring us help and guidance. Guides will organise meaningful meetings and cause us to be in the right place at the right time. Angels of synchronicity, with their access to levity, will cause happy coincidences or agreements in time to aid the smooth running of our daily lives. Our trust in these synchronicities and success in invoking the angels of synchronicity can, incidentally, be a barometer of our openness to positive influences.

The car parking angels who are also angels of synchronicity are among my favourites. Like many angels they give their guidance by activating and inspiring our intuitive function. When I give these angels due warning of my needs and open my intuition to receive their direction, I easily find a suitable space when I need to park my car. Once, going to a restaurant in a busy area on a wet and windy night, I had assured a doubting male friend that there would be a space outside our destination for his extremely long and difficult-to-park car. As we arrived, a rather short car pulled out. Ignoring his snort of derision and imploring the angels not to fail me, I asked him to pull forward and wait a moment. Sure enough a second car pulled out, leaving us the perfect space.

This phenomenon happens with such reliability that I, and friends who also invoke the blessing of the car parking angels, *know* that a force is working with us. If it can work for car parking it can – and does – work in other areas of life too. The angels of trust and synchronicity work very closely together.

The angels of transmutation

These are angels which deserve a special mention. Since it was Gildas who first brought them to my attention, I leave him to speak:

'Angels of transmutation do a special work. They take the darknesses of life and reweave them into substance of light. You can visualise them working with a great lake of dark matter, gradually purifying it and making it light so that it can be used in the healing of individuals, nations and the substance of earth itself.

'These angels cannot take away the dark matter which you often carry until it is freely and willingly handed over.

'When you are facing negative emotions, guilt is almost always a part of the picture. Guilt causes you to hold on to the negativity, feeling your pain and your bitter regrets over and over again. Holding on can hold back your spiritual progress by locking you into the past. It can delay self-forgiveness and the healing of your self-image. At such times you need the angels of transmutation. Openly hand over to them all your pain and regrets. They will welcome your gift with love. From its heaviness they will weave new substance of light.

'On the spiritual path, worry about negative emotions is common. Psychologically, you are told not to repress anger because unless it is released it will fester, cause resentments or illogical behaviour and block creativity. Spiritually you are taught that negative thoughts can become thought forms or entities and take on a life of their own.

'The angels of transmutation can resolve this dilemma. As part of catharsis, call on the transmutation angels. Ask them to accept and transmute the negativity or anger which you are ready to release.

'The angels of transmutation work eventually, to

their own redundancy. When every last bit of negativity has been released and reclaimed, their task will be over. They will then move on, joyfully, to different fields of endeavour.

'Angels of transmutation differ from angels of transformation. The former take the dark substance and work to change its essence. The latter use spiritual grace in their work, instantly changing patterns before they become heavily etched in either the personal or the collective etheric web (see Glossary). Only a proportion of darkness or negativity can be transformed. Most of it must be transmuted.

'When the angels of transmutation have left, lovingingly carrying the negative substance which will further their work, the angels of transformation take over. They ensure an insurge of new energy so that no vacuum is left after cathartic release. Angels of transformation and transmutation work closely together.'

The simplest, most comprehensive, invocation of all

When you are busy or stressed, you may find it difficult to name the particular angels you need. You may be frustrated by the necessity to choose. It is a human trait to ignore the very help which is easily available, when you are most in need.

At such times, try to remember to say simply: 'I invoke the presence and aid of the angels of light and love and healing'. All angels, despite their more specific titles, work under these three broad headings. With this invocation the angels you need will come to your support and aid.

How angels communicate

At first, when working with guides, you must be ready for the subtle ways in which they use life and synchronicity to answer your questions and demonstrate their care. If you are patient and persistent in forging the contact with them, they will also teach you to develop a specific and clear way of receiving their communication. Usually this will be through words received like dictation, either written down or spoken out loud into a tape recorder. They may introduce thoughts immediately into your mind or provide you with symbols to interpret or with which you can work.

Angels rarely have such a direct means of communication. They work most commonly through synchronicity. They will remind you of their presence in a flash of light or colour, or by instilling a happy or creative thought into your mind. They will subtly inspire, comfort and give protection to you, your loved ones, your property.

Occasionally they will put words into your head or give you a snatch of poetry. These direct messages have a different quality from those of the guides. Taking an analogy of bells, angels have the higher, clearer, tinkling notes, while guides have the deeper, resonant tones.

Exercise 10
Angel Cards

There are some delightful, commercially produced, small angel cards, each bearing the name of an angelic quality with a tiny humorous illustration (see Bibliography).

A useful exercise in getting to know angels is to make your own angel card set. When you have read this chapter, reflect seriously on the patterns of your life and make the list of angels you most need. Be creative. There is an angel for each human quality. Neither the list given here nor that of any published angel cards can be comprehensive.

Though you may not be able to make illustrations, try to make the cards attune to the spirit of angels. Use coloured card. Take time to cut it well. Your whole angel set should be on one colour. Use some gold and silver gummed stars for decorations and brightness. Remember to buy plenty of card as you will probably want to add to your pack as you get used to inviting specific angels into your life.

Once you have made your cards there are a number of ways in which they may be used.

(a) Put them face down, mentally ask for the angel which has a message for you and select a card intuitively. Meditate on the angel you have chosen, asking for insights into your life. The angel of humour may tell you to take things more lightly or that you are the one who can relieve an otherwise tense situation by using your gift of humour; the angel of responsibility may tell you that he is there to help lighten your burden of responsibilities, or remind you that you are taking too much responsibility for something or someone. The angels with lighter titles are there to remind you to move from gravity to levity. Remember to have plenty of cards for the angels who will bring more fun, laughter and celebration.

(b) In a meditative way, consider each angel card you have made. Decide which you most need as an ally. Try to limit yourself to choosing only one, but if this is really difficult do not use more than three. Limiting your choice in this way will help you to be more certain about what may be at the root of the particular situation or life phase for which you are seeking support.

When you have made your choice, put your angel(s) somewhere where you can constantly be reminded of its/their blessing and succour.

(c) If you have a puzzling dream, place the cards face down and intuitively choose an angel who will help to clarify its meaning for you.

(d) If you want to incubate a dream for guidance, place the cards face down and intuitively choose the angel who will, in co-operation with your guides, bless and bring the dream to you. Use the 'sacred rule of three' by asking the angel three times to inspire your dreaming self to bring you insight. (For more on dreams and guidance see page 99.)

(e) Intuitively choose cards from the face-down pack for each of your family. Put the cards, still face down, near the family's plates at a meal time and discover which angels are helping each individual, and which are co-operating to help you all as a unit.

(f) Similarly, put a basket of cards on the meal table and let each member of the family intuitively choose their own angel for the day or the coming week.

(g) If a family or group has a problem to be discussed or resolved, begin by asking everyone quietly and intuitively to take an angel who will offer each individual, as well as the group, special support and insight.

(h) At New Year or on a birthday, intuitively choose an angel for the year or for each month of the coming year. Write the names of the chosen angels down and note how they oversee the pattern of your life as the year passes.

(i) Invent a new way to use your angel cards!

Exercise 11
Activating a Personal Angel Crystal

Crystals focus and amplify. Activating a personal angel crystal will help you to focus more easily on the angels you need at any given time and will amplify your receptivity to their guidance.

A small, clear quartz or piece of rose quartz crystal is ideal for this purpose. When you have acquired it, either by buying or receiving it as a gift, wash it well, under cold running water and then breathe on it three times in order to cleanse and prepare it for use.

Design a simple ceremony in which you light a candle, invoke the help of your guides, and the angels of light, love and healing. Speak a few clear words of dedication either aloud or mentally. For example:'I dedicate this crystal to be a bridge between myself and the angelic streams of consciousness. I ask that it may make my contact with angels more vivid and activate my receptivity to their protection and guidance'.

Whenever you feel in need of angelic support, hold your crystal as you invoke the appropriate angels. Touch it often, simply as a reminder that angels are always near.

As you acquire crystals you can use the cleansing method described above to prepare them for use. This should be repeated from time to time to keep your crystal clear and active. If you have Tibetan bells or a Tibetan singing bowl, the sounds from these will also cleanse and clear crystals.

For a thorough cleansing and reactivation of crystals you can soak them in sea salt water for three days before the full moon, dry them on silk and put them on a windowsill or in the garden on the night of the full moon. (It does not matter if the moon is obscured by cloud.)

After this, they should be thoroughly recharged by receiving hours of direct sunlight. (Fortunately for those living in Britain, this does not have to be continuous.) Your crystals are then ready for dedication and use.

This last method is not suitable for soft and flaky crystals, synthetic crystals, or those which are mounted in silver or gold settings.

7

GUIDES, ANGELS AND HEALING FOR OURSELVES AND THE PLANET

> Channelling healing ... Healing with colour ...Absent or distant healing ... Family healing ... Healing for birth, death and life transitions ... Healing for governments, races, cities and groups ... Healing the earth and the balance between species ... Healing the universe ... Exercise 12.

Channelling healing

The word 'channelling' has become associated with bringing guidance through from other worlds or dimensions. Yet many art forms might also be seen as types of channelling. Artists, poets, writers, musicians, actors and actresses, architects, designers, comforters of the sick and troubled are all inspired. They channel enlightenment from beyond themselves which they endeavour to capture and express for the benefit, or entertainment, of others, as well as for their fulfilment.

Guides and angels take an unseen part in many inspired communication forms. The art and science of healing is included. True healers, whether they be doctors, nurses, acupuncturists, herbalists, homoeopaths, therapists or layers-on of hands are all supported by invisible helpers and channel healing power. The energy and flow of healing is freely available in the universe.

The ability to heal is in each one of us. Even if you do not wish, or intend, to become a professional healer, you can still use this gift effectively to help those around you. Often we use it naturally, without giving it the label of healing. Parents touch and soothe their fevered children. We gently bathe wounds or lovingly prepare a 'little something' to tempt a poor appetite. We plump pillows, smooth sheets and hold or caress each other when illness strikes. These are instinctual healing reactions which can easily and safely be developed, and given more structure.

When we channel healing we automatically draw our guides and angels close. They inspire and direct the healing flow and employ us as the necessary transforming bridge across which healing energy must come in order to be used by the physical body. A simple image for healing is to imagine a car with a lifeless battery (the sick person). In order to get the car started, jump leads (the healer) have to be connected between a car with a strong battery (the energy source) and the one which will not start.

It is important to remember that the healer is not the energy source (strong battery), but the bridge or channel (jump leads) through which the energy travels to become available to the place where it is needed (weak battery).

When we are in reasonable health we recharge our own batteries by resting or taking part in some revitalising activity. When we are ill we temporarily lose this ability and need healing energy to be transmitted to us.

Many people find it difficult to imagine attuning to, and channelling from, the vast diffuse resource of healing in the universe. When we have a concept of guides and angels we have a focus. Invocation and prayer to our guide or the angels whom we can name, inspires us with confidence to channel healing.

As mentioned above (see also page 75), you can simply invoke the angels of light, love and healing when you need to connect with angelic inspiration. A named angel can engender a greater sense of focus. The Archangel Raphael inspires healers and comforts those who are sick in body, mind or spirit.

Your healing guides, when asked, will also direct and inspire the healing flow. You do not have to be advanced in guidance work or channelling to be able to make the simple request which will bring the required, albeit unseen, support.

Before you begin to channel healing, wash your hands and do Exercise 12 on grounding.

Invoke your healing guide, the angels of light, love and healing, and the inspiration of the Archangel Raphael. Visualising a deep rosy red colour or having it in the room where you are working attracts Raphael's presence and blessing.

Make sure that your 'patient' is sitting or lying comfortably and can easily be touched when you reach out with your hands.

Rub your hands together briskly for a few moments. Hold your hands just above the head or shoulders, and ask your patient's higher self to receive and use the healing offered in the best possible way for that person at this time. Ask their guardian angel to oversee the giving and receiving of the healing flow.

Put your hands lightly on the parts where your patient needs healing or hold them just slightly above the body at these sites. Let your attunement and your intuition direct your hands, and 'tell' you when enough energy has been received. (You cannot 'overdose' with healing – especially if you have made the above acknowledgement of the patient's higher self.) Quite quickly, you will develop the ability to sense when the healing flow has eased or is no longer being absorbed.

If you do not want to put your hands on or over the body, just rest them lightly on the patient's shoulders or head and breathe through your heart chakra (see Glossary).

When you feel the flow is diminishing, or after 15 to 20 minutes, step back and visualise your patient enclosed in an egg of bright white light. Visualise a separate egg of white light surrounding you. This is called 'making an energetic separation' and is very important. During the healing your energies mingle with those of your patient and, at the end, each of you needs to be firmly in your own space once more. The egg around the patient also ensures that the healing will continue to be absorbed. If you find visualisation difficult just say aloud, or mentally, 'I enclose you in an egg of bright white light, and myself in a separate egg of bright white light, and ask our guides and the Archangel Raphael to aid our energetic separation.'

Healing with colour

If you enjoy this experience of healing and when you feel more confident, you may like to visualise colour as part of the healing process. As you make progress with receiving information from your guides you can ask them to give you advice as to the specific healing colours to use. Remember that all healing colour is bright, light and translucent, having the appearance of stained glass when sunlight passes through it. Make it a guidance exercise to receive either the vision or name of the colours you need to use. Alternatively, trust your intuition to reveal this information.

Cherubim are the guardians and producers of all light and colour. Invoke the Cherubim before visualising colours for healing. Do not be afraid to experiment with colour visualisations. The worst that can happen if you get it wrong is that the patient's aura will reject, or fail to absorb, the colour being offered. Asking the higher self to use the colour healing in the best way for the patient, should be observed, as before (see page 82). More knowledge about colour is required before attempting to use physical sources such as coloured bulbs or lights.

The following is a brief guide to the meaning and use of colour in healing.

- **Red**   Should be modified to the deep pink tones which aid grounding and boost vitality. Deep reddish pinks put us in touch with our bodies and instincts, and activate our self-healing mechanisms. They heal the substance of the body (bones, flesh and malfunctioning organs).
- **Orange**   Use the apricot and amber tones of orange when healing. All shades of orange encourage vitality, activate creativity, heal sexuality, aid self-confidence and the building of a positive self-image. The orange colours heal the water element in the body (blood, colds, catarrh, genito-urinary infections and disorders).
- **Yellow**   The colour of confidence, focus and mental ability. Modified to a sunshiny gold it heals the digestion and the eyes.
- **Green**   Is for compassion, wisdom, detachment and tenderness. It soothes and quietens, and is helpful to breathing difficulties and the circulatory system.
- **Blue**   Is the colour of communication, expression, purpose and general healing. It helps to lower fever, and is particularly good for throat and ear complaints.
- **White**   Purifies and cleanses, spiritually, emotionally and physically. It is particularly effective where there has been food poisoning or over-exposure to sunlight.
- **Rose pink**   Brings comfort, and is excellent for healing babies and very young children.

The visualisation of colour can also be used in self-healing. It will attract extra angelic blessings for your healing endeavours.

Absent or distant healing

This form of healing works extremely well. If you know someone in need of healing but are unable to visit them, arrange to have a quiet time in which you 'think' healing energy towards them or 'hold them in the light'.

Light a candle and have your healing crystals with you.

Do the grounding exercise on page 91. Invoke the help of your guide, the angels of light and love and healing, and specifically the Virtues. These angels respond to prayers and requests for healing. They direct concentrations of divine energy into particular areas or towards named individuals.

Say aloud, three times, the name of the person for whom you are requesting healing. Imagine them surrounded with golden light. After about five minutes' concentration, see them fit, well and following their favourite pursuits.

Healing for world situations, houses or places, can also be part of absent healing using a similar procedure.

You can extend and amplify this healing ceremony by lighting a small candle or night-light for each person or concern to which healing is being sent. At the end, as you extinguish the light or lights, think of sending out the light, rather than putting a candle out. See streams of light flowing towards those to whom healing has been given.

Family healing

Most of us experience disturbing periods of family misunderstandings or eruptions. An increasing number of us endure divorce or broken relationships. We worry about the effects of such trauma on our children.

Within some families relationships become severely damaging. In social work terminology these are known as 'dysfunctional families'. Discoveries of, and admissions about, sexual and physical abuse in families has grown more common.

The wider human family, with its strife between nations, religions, political parties and inhumanity of human to human, is extremely dysfunctional. More and more people are asking not only how to help themselves, but how to help humanity. Distressed by newsreels of wars, knowing that we cannot all rush out there to help, Gildas has been asked: 'We can contribute money, but that is not enough. What can we do on subtle levels that will really help?'

Guides, as well as angels, belong to groups, each of which works, in close co-operation with the angels, to a particular purpose. Invoke a guide to oversee healing for your immediate family or for the family of nations. If your contact with one direct guide is strong, then that guide will be able to have prior consultation with the angels and the group of guides who oversee this area of healing. They will then guide you as to the colours, crystals and fragrances which would be most effective as healing aids. The Archangel Gabriel concerns himself with healing for nuclear families and for the wider family of humanity as a whole.

One member of an immediate family, working alone, can activate effective healing. If other family members work with you, it becomes a more co-operative and supportive venture, though not necessarily more effective or powerful in terms of the healing channelled. Likewise, one member of the greater human family can also work powerfully, alone. Nevertheless it is also worth while to share a sense of purpose and concern, and channel the wider healing with a small group. If this is difficult to organise, arranging to 'tune in' with a friend or a few other people at a prearranged time is also usefully supportive.

The magic hours

There are certain hours at which it is particularly powerful to send out absent healing. A well-known guide called White Eagle spoke of these as the 'magic hours'. They were used by light workers during the Second World War. They are the hours of 3, 6, 9 and 12 throughout the 24-hour day. It makes no difference which time zone you happen to be in, because angels and guides are beyond time and can synchronise with us. Wherever these particular hours are observed, guides and angels are enabled to have a more 'direct line' to our earth plane and consciousness.

When healing your immediate family it is a good idea to light a night-light for each family member, saying their names mentally or aloud as you do so. Arrange the lights in a circle, representing the family as a whole, but respecting each personality within it. To help in the invocation to Gabriel, have the colour green represented in the room where you are working, or visualise a fresh spring green, as you invoke: 'The angels of light and love and healing, my own guides, those guides who oversee the healing of families, and particularly the Archangel Gabriel.'

Concentrate quietly on your family, visualising it functioning happily rather than focusing on its difficulties. You can say a simple prayer for each member, such as 'Help Michael', 'Bless Margaret', or you can visualise each family member surrounded in light.

After 10 to 15 minutes, thank the angels and guides for their presence. Blow out the candles, sending out the light to each family member for whom they were lit. Surround yourself with a cloak and hood of white light.

Healing for births, deaths and life transitions

Being incarnate involves us in constant change. So-called 'primitive societies' recognise, mark and celebrate life's rites of passage with appropriate, often colourful ceremonies and rituals.

Marking beginnings and endings as an acknowledgement of change can be physically, emotionally, mentally and spiritually beneficial.

Birth and death are the most obvious and important rites of passage. In recent years there has been less public shame about the processes of birth. Death is no longer an unmentionable subject. It is more common to have discussions with those who are dying about their funeral arrangements. Traditional funeral services are being replaced by valedictory celebrations of the life which has ended. Inappropriate 'pomp and circumstance' is waning. Positive progress is being made.

Other life changes such as coming of age and marriage

have their own celebratory customs. Usually insufficient reference to the spiritual dimension is included. Moving to a new life phase means new responsibilities. Ceremonies which truly acknowledge the sacred activate spiritual resources within the psyche and imbue new undertakings with a reverential quality. When these elements are lacking, responsibility too easily becomes something to be feared or for which we feel spiritually inadequate.

Life transitions such as puberty, divorce, moving house, menopause and retirement are rarely fittingly or sufficiently marked. Children's rites of passage suffer a similar fate. Birthdays are usually celebrated, but other life transitions to new beds or bedrooms, acquiring a new brother or sister, starting school, loosing milk teeth and changing schools, are all signposts on the journey to maturity. Honouring them deals with any mourning or regrets about the phase which has passed and makes it clear that a new phase with new obligations but also new privileges is being entered.

Designing and celebrating rite of passage ceremonies can be fun and rewarding. Honouring the spiritual element without getting too heavy about it is an area where the angels love to add their expertise.

The Powers are the angels in the hierarchy who inspire human consciousness and higher ideals. They oversee the rhythms of birth, death and rebirth.

These angels can be called upon to bless rites of passage. They will calm parents' fears before the birth of a child, liaising with its guardian angel, as well as with those of its parents.

Solace for the dying, comfort for the bereaved, and the bringing of beauty, joy and dignity to funerals or valedictory services are all overseen by the Powers.

The Archangel Gabriel gives particular protection to families, women and children. He can be invoked to bring especial blessing to family rituals and to women's rites of passage.

If there is a life stage or transition you and your family would like to mark in a special way, invoke the blessing and guidance of the Powers and/or the Archangel Gabriel. (See page 26 for advice on formal invocation.)

Healing for governments, nations, races, cities and groups

The angels known as Principalities are overseers and guardians of large groups, organisations, nations, races and cities. They promote loyalty, wise leadership, maturity and sane, peaceful interactions. They enhance the potential of all co-operative human ventures.

You can assist the Principalities to focus their healing for a troubled nation; a government faced with the immense dilemmas of the world of today; your own race scattered, as most are now, all over the globe; your city, that its history and beauties be preserved or that its trouble spots be calmed; or for any group to which you belong. (This could be the workforce, team or network with whom you work, just as well as a political, spiritual, leisure time, or task group.)

Refer to the absent healing section on page 84. Create a similar ritual for working with the Principalities. Remember that your prayers or invocations to them act as a bridge, so that the energies they produce and the work in which they specialise can be fully earthed and directed to where required.

Healing the earth and the balance between species

One of the most emotive issues must be that of animal rights. Concerted protest and insistence on better standards shows increasing awareness of the animal kingdoms and the responsibilities we have to all forms of life. Nothing which lives can exist in total self-sufficiency. There is an interdependency between, as well as within, species. Even parasitic creatures and plants usually perform a service for the host from which they feed.

One of the areas where humanity has gone most astray in our relationship to nature, is in dishonouring the balances between species and within the substance of earth itself. We have interfered with natural equilibrium and basic rhythms. We are worried about global warming, the ozone layer and genus extinction. Gildas and other guides have indicated that we have not yet begun to understand the implications of our failure to protect creatures such as whales and dolphins. The sounds which these and other animals make are part of the harmony of the earth. When those sounds are insufficient, missing or changed, then the ozone layer fails and faults in the earth's crust are further weakened.

The angels which aid our understanding of nature, and renew our reverence for the earth and all life are the Thrones and the Powers.

The Throne angels work to counteract our insensitivity to the environment. They welcome co-operation from individuals and groups. Increased awareness, prayer and invocation, augment their work and support their endeavours.

The Powers inspire human consciousness and higher ideals. They oversee morphic resonance (see page 22), ensuring that the positive waves created by light-working individuals and groups vibrate at least ten times more strongly than would otherwise be possible. Increased resonance causes positive changes in the behaviour patterns of a species. If we are ever to achieve the full potential which includes harmony with all life forms, we must call upon the Powers.

When working to channel healing for the earth and for balance between species, invoke the Thrones (particularly the Earth Throne) and the Powers.

Healing the universe

As we become more aware that the earth is one dot within a vast universe, our healing endeavours must take on wider and wider perspectives. As we heal the earth, we also contribute to universal healing. When we hold the highest vision for interplanetary communication and co-operation we support the work of the higher angelic realms.

The collection of orbiting objects which we have abandoned in space are bound to have an adverse effect on the sacred geometrical precision required for interplanetary balance and harmony. We need, therefore, to co-operate, through healing, with the angelic forces responsible for holding and correcting universal balance.

This particular healing and invocation is especially effective when practised by a small group. Consider the possibilities there might be for working outdoors on a clear night, especially on a hilltop where there is a wide vista of the night sky and the heavenly bodies.

The Seraphim conduct the music of the spheres, and keep the correct balance, alignment and movement between planets, stars and other heavenly bodies.

If you organise or become part of such a group, invoke the Seraphim and offer yourselves as participants in the healing of the universe. Dancing sacred or circle dances as part of the healing ceremonial is an effective way to include harmony, as well as to mirror and awaken consciousness of sacred rhythms and movements.

Exercise 12
Grounding and Clearing as a Preparation for Healing Work (two versions)

First version

Stand with your spine straight and your body balanced. Consciously release any tension you are carrying, particularly in your joints. Loosen your knees, waist, elbows and shoulders. Shake your head, to release tension in your neck.

Begin by being aware of the rhythm of your breathing and letting it slow down a little. Imagine a breath coming from just above the crown of your head, draw it down through the centre of your body. Change to the out-breath at a point which feels natural for you, and breathe out as though right down and through your legs, into the earth.

On the next inhalation breathe up from the earth, through the centre of your body, letting the out-breath go out through the crown of your head.

Continue to breathe in this way, without straining or forcing, for about five minutes. Always end on the downward sequence. Feel the balance in your body as you begin to give the healing for which you have prepared.

Second version

Begin by releasing tensions from your joints as in First version, above. Become aware of your breathing rhythm, let it steady and slow down.

Visualise yourself as a tree. Your branches stretch out above, your roots plunge deeply into the earth, your trunk is straight and strong. You are nurtured by the four elements. Sun (fire) warms you and air refreshes you; your roots are fed by the earth, and watered by underground streams and sources of living water.

Breathe in through your branches, from the elements of air and sun, take the breath right down through your trunk and breathe out strongly into your roots, into the earth, into the streams of living water.

Now breathe in from the earth and the living water, bring the breath up through your roots, through your trunk, into your branches, and breathe out into the elements of air and sun.

Repeat these two breath sequences for five to ten minutes. Gradually let the visualisation fade. Feel your feet firmly on the ground, your own space all around you and begin to give the healing for which you have prepared yourself.

8

GUIDES IN DAILY LIFE

Strengthening and developing contact with a guide ...
Pendulums ... Establishing a routine ... Reaching the
right level for guidance ... Keeping a guide book ...
Making life reviews ... Asking the right question ...
Dreams as guidance ... Symbols ... Channelling for a
friend or partner ... Higher self, inner wisdom or
discarnate guide? ... Psychic protection from unwanted
entities and influences ... Exercises 13 and 14.

Strenthening and developing contact
with a guide

Guides are equally as present as angels in their care of us.
Most have a wonderful sense of humour, often urging us to
take life more lightly. Nevertheless, our main connection
with them needs to be more planned and formal than does
our contact with angels.

Angels come to us on a very distinct stream of light
consciousness which is separate from the human stream.
They work for the manifestation and realisation of divine
principles. They are concerned with the universe, earth and
humans – though they are not human (see also Chapter 3).
Some of the problems which beset the work with guides are
not present in our contact with angels because of the nature
of their vibration and the subtle ways in which they
communicate with us as a part of daily living.

Guides, though discarnate and having the wider perspective of life seen from other planes, are essentially human. They have evolved and are still evolving according to the pattern of humanity. They come from planes where there is activity and interaction between different manifestations and levels of being. In technical terms, the lines on which they communicate with us are full of 'noise'.

Angels bless us and lend their energies to making our lives more positive. Guides will listen to all we would tell them of the smallest details of our lives. Having listened, they give advice. Here lies a danger. Most human beings have difficulty in making choices. We easily become dependent on guidance. We too readily bow to authority or hand over responsibility. We are afraid of doing the wrong thing but also addicted to having our progress evaluated.

I see many people in the first flush and excitement of guidance, expecting their guides to live their lives for them. They will ask about everything, no longer trusting their own wisdom, intelligence or intuition; no longer open to taking even the smallest risks or learning from personal experience. Some cases are extreme.

Pendulums

During the search for guidance most people discover that a pendulum can be used to obtain a response to questions which have a 'yes' or 'no' answer (see Glossary). Through attunement, guides will inspire or control a pendulum which, wisely used, can be a helpful tool. On the other hand pendulum work is open to interference and may feed the wrong kind of addiction to guidance.

The worlds of guidance offer the seductions of glamour and escapism. Believing in guides almost presupposes a belief in other lifetimes and reincarnation. There are times when insight into previous lives will clarify, and help us to resolve, the problems of the present. At other times, our interest in our personal past may be motivated at best by simple curiosity, at worst by narcissism, inflation or a desire for power. Using guides as a means of feeding these latter motivations can be dangerous. Using guides as a means of obtaining facile information about the evolution of our friends or enemies, especially without their knowledge or permission, is grossly indiscreet. A higher guide will require good reasons for looking into such information and will never give it as a matter of course.

Beyond our self-centred concerns, guides have many interesting perspectives and much captivating information to offer. They encourage us to look at life's dilemmas in new ways. They give fascinating teachings about cosmology, healing, other planes and the eternity of existence. Asking more philosophical questions accelerates the development of higher guidance and avoids many of the pitfalls encountered in receiving answers to personal emotional dilemmas (see page 43). Receiving such teaching is not something which most people would wish to experience every day. This is an advantage. Limiting contact with guides to specific times, together with a refusal to trivialise the contents of the interactions, has the paradoxical effect of strengthening our sense of our guides' presence and companionship. They become real friends in a relationship of mutual respect instead of being used as excuses for playing with the phenomena of other planes and realities.

Establishing a routine

The exercises for establishing guidance which have already been given are the basic tools required. Using these regularly will bring results. Some people inevitably progress more quickly than others. When you feel stuck, rereading Chapter 5 will remind you of the work required, the possible hazards and the allies to be called upon when clearing blockages. As the contact strengthens, most guides will take a lively part in your training, setting new tasks and exercises, and giving fresh insights.

Decide how much time you can reasonably dedicate to the work of establishing guidance. Every day, even for practising the exercises, does not necessarily bring quicker results. Over-enthusiasm can cause you to impose unrealistic expectations on yourself about the frequency with which you can arrange practice sessions. Be wary. Each time you fail to meet your self-imposed schedule you will build in a sense of failure. It is far better to have a minimal expectation which also allows you to take advantage of unexpected opportunities for working. In this way you will build sound foundations and enjoy a sense of success or incrementation on each occasion where you take steps to develop your guidance contact.

Reaching the right level for guidance

Emphasis has been placed on the journey you need to make in order to achieve the level of consciousness which enables a safe meeting place with your highest guide (see page 62). Sometimes people take this instruction so seriously that they aim too high. They report a beautiful or blissful sense of another dimension, often with bright light and colour. They are aware of higher beings but everything is nebulous and a true guidance connection is not achieved.

If this happens, greater concentration on the heart chakra is required. Learning to bring the higher energy through the heart prevents any tendency to soar to levels of mystical experience when seeking contact with a discarnate guide. Higher guides may accompany you to the higher mental planes where mystical perceptions take place, but the initial meeting level with guides is on the feeling or lower mental planes (see Glossary). As you progress in the spiritual life, clear definition of your level of working will enable precision and safety in finding that which you seek. Exercise 11 will help in bringing higher energies to the level of the heart chakra.

Keeping a guide book

It is a good idea to keep a book in which you record the results of your exercises in guidance, together with notes of any difficulties or reactions. Times, dates and places will help you to recognise or plot your progress, and to be aware of such things as the best time of day, the best location and the most powerful times of each month or year for your work. For instance, some people find that they work best at certain phases of the moon.

In your guide book you can also record questions you have asked and questions you intend to ask. It can be used for recording your dreams and the results of any life reviews you decide to make.

Making life reviews

When working with guides and angels the making of regular life reviews is a useful tool. Monthly, on a certain date, works well.

Gildas once said that the secret of effective living, both spiritually and materially is to 'be present'. Often our thoughts are engaged with the immediate or distant future, or absorbed by past events. In the present we are vague, forgetful and unobservant. It is a telling reflection on life that most people will agree that the knowledge of moments of happiness is most often registered in retrospect. 'I was happy then,' we will say, recognising that we did not fully identify, or bask in, that quality at the time. Modern life can be so goal-oriented that we rush on towards the horizon without enjoying or appreciating the landscape around us.

Life reviews are not about dwelling on the past, but about making trends and patterns more conscious. If you know that you are going to make a life review, you will begin to notice the things you want to note down as they happen.

As your life reviews build up in your guide book, make a habit of looking back at previous entries. You will soon recognise the subtle ways in which your guides and angels have been present with you in your sorrows and joys, bringing comfort, inspiration and love to make your understanding of the meaning of life more positive and creative.

Emerging from life reviews there will be not only an awareness of how guidance is manifesting for you, but clarity about the questions you need to be asking.

Asking the right question

When we realise how close our guides are, it is tempting to imagine that they will tell us all we need to know, thereby relieving us of the need to find the right questions to ask. This is another version of our reluctance to take self-responsibility. It is also an assumption that guides know all our feelings and views, and hold our destiny in their hands. The higher guides would find it a discourteous invasion to 'read' us in this way.

Guides require a dialogue, especially with the Aquarian guidance model (see page 40). If you have something to discuss with a dear friend, you would consider it a privilege and necessity to have a sympathetic listener as you reveal your innermost feelings in your own way. The golden rule is to treat your guide as a dear friend and express yourself accordingly. When you do so your guide's comments and advice will be more personal, precise and specific. If, in turn, you listen to your guide as you would to a valued friend, you will learn about the difficulties and joys of life on the other side. Contact with guides should never be one-sided. Do not dwell only on your sorrows and problems, express your delights and accomplishments as well as your fears. In this way, the whole of your life will receive the benefit of another perspective and you will be in a two-way mature relationship with your guide.

Finding the right question to ask is an essential part in the development of guidance. Often, identifying an initial question brings the realisation that its answer is already known in your place of inner wisdom. By going through the process whereby one question leads on to the next, you will eventually arrive at the deeper questions which need to be asked.

Exercise 14 will help you find the right question.

Dreams as guidance

Dreams are rich in the guidance which comes from the inner wise places of our psyches. Guides and angels will help us to incubate dreams (see page 77). Sometimes discarnate guides will apear in our dreams if we are unable to contact them in waking consciousness.

Everyone dreams every night though we do not always remember our dreams. If you find it difficult to remember your dreams, recording fragments, or the images and feelings which come just before going to sleep or immediately on waking, will signal to your psyche that you want to listen to its more secret life. Do not struggle to analyse your dreams' content. Begin by keeping a record of dreams or dream fragments in your guide book. Read through these from time to time and gradually the insights they hold will unfold.

Symbols

The language of dreams is puzzling because it is symbolic. As symbols come to you, through dreams or from angels and guides, try to resist the temptation to over-analyse them. As you 'live' with a symbol its layers of meaning will gradually reveal themselves. If you want to read about your symbols, refer to the type of book which gives historical background and the meaning of the particular symbol in different cultures (see Bibliography).

There are some symbol books which make categorical

statements such as 'snake means transformation', but you, and only you, hold the most important clues to interpreting your own symbols. What does this mean to you? If you have a very real fear of snakes and they come into your inner world or dreams, perhaps it will be some time before you can appreciate their transformative aspect. For you, the snake as a symbol may be asking that you work with that fear and identify its source.

The stage of exploring what a symbol means or has meant in your life is called the stage of association. Only when you have explored this fully should you turn to books or others for the next stage which is amplification. Amplification gives you information about the symbol so that you can decide which is relevant to you and your dream or life situation, and which is not.

Symbols are never simplistic in their meaning or significance. Because they are the means whereby the deeper reaches of our psyches speak to us, their wealth of meaning will become accessible only gradually, yet their presence in our consciousness is a gift. Symbols may help us to look at inner difficulties. They may also reveal unsuspected strengths and should be greeted with honour, reverence and excitement.

(Further reading on dreams and symbols is given in the Bibliography.)

Channelling for another person

Mention of the difficulties involved in channelling personal advice for ourselves and those close to us has already been made (see page 43), but when developing the ability to channel, finding a 'working partner' can be useful. Share a dream you have each had and channel some insights or interpretations for each other. Take it in turns to specify a life dilemma and ask the other's guide for a new perspective or symbol. Give each other feedback about the quality and effectiveness of the channelling. Recognising the atmosphere present when your guides come through will develop your awareness of the distinct vibration which each guide has. It is usually clearly perceptible. When you have reassurance about this you will worry less about whether the words or images are your own or your guide's.

Higher self, inner wisdom or discarnate guide?

People often question how to distinguish the origin of their guidance. In the initial phases this is of lesser importance than making sure that what is received is pertinent and has all the qualities of good guidance (see page 43). As experience builds you will identify subtle differences in energy, vibration, tone and direction. Guidance from the higher self often originates from a place just above the crown of the head. Inner wisdom emanates from a place within the body, often just behind the heart centre. The energy of guides is usually felt high up behind, or on the left or right-hand side of the body. Occasionally the guide will 'stand' directly in front of the channel.

Psychic protection from unwanted entities and influences

Some esoteric sources advise the erection of all manner of visualised devices such as psychic mirrors and shields. These are only applicable to specialised work and in some circumstances. If you develop discernment, work at self-knowledge, become aware of all the issues connected with colouring and realise that you must make a journey in consciousness in order to meet with your guide, you will not need psychic protection. In the way of working suggested in this book, protection is an in-built factor. If you do have doubts or difficulties seek advice from a channel, healer or counsellor you trust.

Usually, the only visual protective device I recommend, and

which is included in the exercises given in this book, is the visualisation of a cloak of white light, with a hood, right around you. This encloses you in light and enables you to take light with you wherever you go. It protects you from any over-sensitivity or vulnerability you might experience because of the altered states of consciousness you are entering.

Exercise 13
Bringing Higher Energies into the Heart Chakra

Do the grounding exercise (Exercise 12), followed by the meeting place exercise (Exercise 7). When you are waiting on the plateau, incorporate the following exercise into your waiting time ...

Focus on your heart area. The heart chakra is in the centre of the body on a level with the physical heart ... It is like a flower which can open and close ... As you breathe into the heart chakra, imagine it opening like a rose, petal by petal ... Imagine the fragrance of the rose ... Be aware of a similar energy centre at your throat, another at your brow and another at the crown of your head ... Imagine streams of coloured light from each of the higher centres, flooding down into your heart chakra ... A stream of white light comes from the crown of your head, violet from your brow and blue from your throat ... These colours join with a green and rose flow of light within your heart ... When the flow from the higher chakras to the heart chakra is well established, ask your guide to be present with you and express any questions you wish to ask ...

Make your return journey according to the instructions on page 92.

Exercise 14
Finding the Right Question

Prepare three sheets of paper and some crayons. Making sure that you will be undisturbed sit in a comfortable, but symmetrically balanced position ...

Be aware of the rhythm of your breathing ... Gradually bring that rhythm into your heart centre, so activating your heart chakra energy ...

In the heart energy hold the question: 'Where am I now?' ... Seek an image or symbol as a response to this question ... As it begins to form, start to draw it meditatively, allowing it to develop as you draw ...

Rebalance your body ... reactivate your heart energy by breathing into your heart chakra ...

Ask yourself the question: 'What question should I be asking now?' ... Seek an image or symbol as a response to this question ... As it forms, begin to draw meditatively, using the drawing as further exploration of the image or symbol ...

Consider what you have drawn, as you also explore the above questions mentally and factually.

A FINAL WORD

I hope that you will pursue your work with angels with determination, but also with lightness and humour. Our world of today and the individuals living in it need the beings of light as never before.

Remember that even if your efforts do not produce the vivid results you would like, every aspiration helps to build a bridge of light. As the Golden Age dawns, this bridge will be fully in use in both directions, enabling humans, guides and angels to walk hand in hand, filling the planet with light, love, healing and peace.

GLOSSARY

Aura The energy field, which interpenetrates with, and radiates out beyond, the physical body. Clairvoyantly seen, the aura is full of light, colour and shade. The trained healer or seer sees or senses indications within the aura as to the spiritual, mental, physical and emotional state of the individual. Much of the auric colour and energy comes from the chakras.

Chakras The word '*chakrum*' is Sanskrit and means 'wheel'. Properly speaking, *chakrum* is the singular form and *chakra* the plural, but in the West it is usual to speak of one chakra and many chakras. Clairvoyantly seen they are wheels of light and colour interpenetrating with, affecting and affected by, the physical body. Most chakras carry links to specific parts of the glandular system and might therefore be described as subtle glands. Eastern traditions describe a sevenfold major chakra system, at the same time acknowledging the presence of varying large numbers of minor chakras. The names of the major chakras are: the Crown (at the crown of the head); the Brow (above and between the eyes); the Throat (at the centre of the neck); the Heart (in the centre of the body, on the same level as the physical heart); the Solar Plexus (just under the rib cage); the Sacral (two fingers below the navel); and the Root (in the perineum area).

Chakras from the Solar Plexus upwards are often referred to as 'higher chakras', and the ones below and including the Solar Plexus as 'lower chakras'. These should not be seen as terms of evaluation. They are descriptive of the position of the chakras in relationship to the physical body when upright. There is not a hierarchical system within the chakras; each is part of a team.

There is a central subtle column of energy interpenetrating with the physical body and running from the crown of the head to the perineum (the area midway between the anus and the genitals). Each chakra has petals and a stem. The stems of the Crown and Root chakras are open, and are contained within the central column. The other chakras have petals opening into the auric field at the front and stems at the back. The stems usually stay closed but the petals are flexible, opening and closing, vibrating and turning according to the different life situations encountered. A healthy chakra is a flexible chakra. Where there is disease, the chakra energies become inflexible or actually blocked. Working with the chakras aids physical, mental, emotional and spiritual health.

The seven major chakras carry the colours of the rainbow spectrum; red for the Root; orange for the Sacral; yellow for the Solar Plexus; green for the Heart; blue for the Throat; indigo for the Brow and violet for the Crown. This does not necessarily mean that the chakras *are* these colours, but that they are responsible for producing that colour note within the chakra team and the auric field. Any colour may be 'seen' or sensed in any chakra. It could be said that each chakra has its own full spectrum of colour. The presence, quality and degree of other colours reflects information about ourselves.

Devic beings These are sometimes confused with angels. Devas are good, shining spirits, often perceived as being very tall. Their concern is with trees, rocks, plants, animals and the four elements. They are guardians who work to maintain balance in these realms and in the interaction of humanity with the natural kingdoms.

Discarnate beings This is a term mainly used when speaking of guides and angels. It refers to the non-incarnational state. Discarnate beings usually live on other planes, they are not leading a current earth life and do not have a physical body.

Elementals, fairies, nature spirits Tiny energy beings generally associated with plants, trees, the natural environment and the elements. They appear to those who 'see', as points of light or colour, or in traditional fairy form as the nereids, sylphs, gnomes, elves, undines, goblins and flower fairies.

Since the four elements interact in our physical bodies and largely determine our health patterns, elementals are within us as well as around us. The giving and receiving of energetic healing activates and encourages the elementals to help us to health and harmony.

Elementals are the lowest manifestation in a hierarchy of a different consciousness stream from the human. Above them are devic beings and angels.

Etheric web The etheric layer or plane is the area of subtle energy which is closest to the physical plane. It is the first layer within the auric field and within it there are subtle duplicates of all the physical organs. The etheric web is all around us. Clairvoyantly seen, it is like a gossamer cobweb of golden light. Similar to a cobweb the etheric web can become sticky and sullied with thought forms and negative energies. In our homes and around our bodies this web can be cleansed by imagining a brush filled with light, gently brushing away all stickiness and bringing a new flow of strong light to its strands.

Karma The spiritual law of cause and effect (which defies 'nutshell' definition). 'As you sow, so shall you reap' gives a basic but over-simplified idea. Belief in karma goes alongside belief in reincarnation and personal, progressive evolution. The tendency is to see karma as troublesome limitations, heavy tasks or symbolic debts which need to be worked out within a specific lifetime – but there is also positive karma. Gifts, aptitudes and innate wisdom or knowledge can be seen as positive karmic attributes.

Light workers This is a term used to describe activities such as working with guides and angels and developing an understanding of the subtle realms of light. Groups who join together for meditation, prayer, invocation and communication with guides related to the healing of humanity and the earth often describe themselves as 'light workers'.

Other planes When incarnate, our existence is dependent upon the substance and solidity of the material plane. Yet we are complex beings and if we pause to study the range of our perceptions, not all can be explained by the laws of matter or physics. Many people encounter 'other-worldly phenomena', from near-death experiences to prophetic dreams, from sensing 'atmospheres' in old buildings to telepathic communication with a loved one, either alive or dead.

Esoteric teaching tells us that there are at least six other planes of experience, which are not just phenomena of perception but actual territories. The nearest to us is the etheric plane, which in itself is largely an interface between the material and the astral planes. This latter is divided into a number of layers or regions. The lower astral is largely populated with negative thought forms. (It is probably the region which alcoholics experience when they have the 'DTs' or drug users when they have a 'bad trip'.) The higher levels of the astral plane are where we meet our guides, where there are temples of light and healing, and beautiful, subtle landscapes. We may visit the astral planes in our dreams, each night, as well as being able to travel there in the altered state of consciousness induced by meditation. Beyond the astral plane are the feeling plane, the lower and higher mental planes, and the causal plane. (Names for each of the planes may vary from teacher to teacher; those used here are given by Gildas.)

Pendulums Any kind of weight on the end of a hand-held thread or chain. The simplest pendulum is a needle swinging at the end of a piece of thread. Many people use a neck-lace or pendant for simple pendulum work. Purpose-made pendulums are usually drop shaped or have a point at the bottom. They are made from wood, resin, lead crystal, natural crystal, stone or metal.

Pendulums 'answer' questions to which the answer is either 'yes' or 'no'. They can be used to 'dowse' choices from a list of foods, articles or remedies, or to highlight areas of special interest on maps. They can be useful in finding lost objects.

Pendulums spiral clockwise or anticlockwise and give diagonal or straight line swings to indicate different answers or possibilities. Before experimenting it is wise to ask someone experienced in pendulum work for some guid-ance, since the direction of positive and negative swings varies from person to person and from pendulum to pendu-lum. Using pendulums for guidance can be limiting and open to interference from low-level spirits.

Talisman This is a special, personal object or touch-stone carrying strongly positive, symbolic meaning. A talisman is a link to inner strength and an enhancer of creativity. The inner talisman is used on inner journeys for empowerment when facing unusual or unexpected situations and choices.

Zoroastrianism An ancient Eastern religion founded by the prophet Zoroaster (Zarathustra), and still followed by the Guebres in Iran and the Parsees in India. Its sacred book or document is known as the *Zend-Avesta*.

BIBLIOGRAPHY

Cooper, C.J. *An Illustrated Encyclopaedia of Symbols*, Thames and Hudson

Ferrucci, Pierro (disciple of Assagioli) *What We May Be*, Thorsons

Holbeche, Soozi *The Power of Your Dreams*, Piatkus Books

Holbeche, Soozi *The Power of Gems and Crystals*, Piatkus Books

Jung, C.G. *Man and His Symbols*, Aldus Books

White, Ruth *A Question of Guidance*, C.W. Daniel Co Ltd

White, Ruth *Working With Your Chakras*, Piatkus Books

White, Ruth *A Message of Love*, Piatkus Books

White, Ruth *The River of Life*, Piatkus Books

White, Ruth and Swainson, Mary *Gildas Communicates*, C.W. Daniel Co Ltd

White, Ruth and Swainson, Mary *The Healing Spectrum*, C.W. Daniel Co Ltd

Angel Cards (page 76) are available from the Findhorn Publishing Company.

INDEX